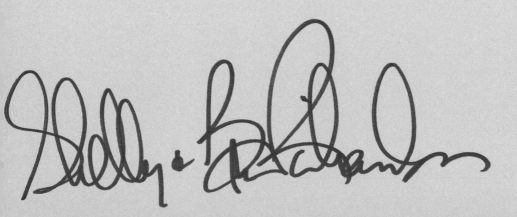

For Moira

A Tea For All Seasons

Celebrating Tea, Art and Music
at the Elmwood Inn

Shelley and Bruce Richardson

Photography by Bruce Richardson

Acknowledgments

We often look at the credits in cookbooks and wonder about the professional crews who work behind the scenes putting a cookbook together. This is our second book and we have learned to appreciate the hard work that goes into a book project. We also know how to produce a book on a limited budget. We have no research assistant, food stylist, professional photographer, set designer, lighting professional, florist, publicist, or typist. Our production staff consists of three people, each wearing several hats.

Shelley was the design leader on this book. She planned the monthly events, coordinated the production schedule, arranged the flowers from her gardens, cooked many of the foods, and worked with all the artists.

Debbie Wheat is our pastry chef and recipe developer. Debbie is not only a culinary artist, she also contributed a sunflower watercolor and a painted floor cloth for our celebration of tea and the arts. Many of the recipes in this book have come from her files. She loaned us fabrics and accessories from her own collection. Her artistic flair often made the difference between an ordinary shot and a spectacular setting. Besides all that, she's a wonderful friend to have in the kitchen.

Bruce did all the photography, musical selections, and the manuscript preparation. He often volunteered as an official new recipe taster.

We owe a great debt to all of the artists who contributed the works for this book. They worked on tight deadlines and carried many paintings in and out of the inn. Many of them did full exhibits at the inn for our guests. Julia Weinstein of Julia's Gallery introduced us to the work of Carol Henry and Elizabeth Murray. You will find all of these talented friends listed in the resource section of this book. You are welcome to contact them for more information on their work.

Margaret Lane was in charge of children, small animals, and encouragement. Thanks also to Betty Hensley for her framing, flowers, and fresh produce. Alan Hoeweler and Mary Breeding were kind enough to let us photograph our July scene in the Karrick-Parks House. Their work with the Perryville Enhancement Project is ensuring the opportunity for future generations to enjoy this historic area.

Friends in the tea business such as John Harney, James Norwood Pratt, and Jane Pettigrew have helped light our path along the way of tea. We are honored to call them friends.

Our publisher, Bill Butler, took a chance on us when we presented him with our first book manuscript back in 1993. That was before he knew that there was such a thirst for tea books. He has now been converted.

Our greatest appreciation goes out to the thousands of people across the country who bought our first book, *A Year of Teas at the Elmwood Inn*, and to all of our wonderful guests who come back month after month for their cup of serenity.

—Shelley & Bruce Richardson

Preface

The changing of the seasons has long been a familiar theme found in sculpture, art, literature and music. Being musicians, one of our favorite depictions of the seasons is found in Antonio Vivaldi's orchestral concertos, The Four Seasons. The images of chirping birds in the spring, threatening thunderstorms in the summer, hunters in autumn, and icy landscapes in the winter are as vivid today as they were when the music was first published in 1725.

Like a recurring theme, this seasonal motif steadily weaves its way through our celebrations of afternoon tea at Elmwood Inn. Our tea menu, always built around a central idea, draws on an eclectic mix of culinary traditions. The seasons play a big part in the design of our tea trays. We use as many fresh fruits and vegetables as possible in our recipes; therefore, strawberries and asparagus find their way to our table in the spring, while blackberries and blueberries are summer tea-time delicacies.

This attention to seasonal details doesn't end in the kitchen. We are fortunate to have many artist friends who are eager to share their wealth of talents with our guests at the inn. We have found that the seasons also influence our choice of art to exhibit in the tea room. August sometimes invites sunflowers, while June lends itself to a rose garden theme. Paintings of angels are often found in December and spring flowers are hung on our walls in May. Seven of these artists have contributed works for this book.

Russian artist Irina Ilina is one of our most frequent exhibitors. Our permanent collection contains several of her works. We commissioned Irina to paint the four lead-in pictures for the seasons of this book. Her captivating portraits set the stage for the wonderful montage of visual, culinary and musical delights which follow.

This book grew out of our deep love for the arts and tea. For us, life is art. We are artists when we design a garden, arrange a bouquet of flowers, choose our clothes, decorate a room, or cook a meal. We are artists even when we prepare a pot of tea.

Throughout the book, we refer to the ritual of taking tea as a "celebration." For many tea lovers, this act of sipping tea with friends in a serene setting surrounded by beautiful art, fresh flowers, delightful foods and great music takes on a spiritual significance not unlike entering a cathedral. This feeling is a sense of enchantment which people long for in our fast-paced society. Ideally, the tea room can become a sanctuary for weary souls, and for many, time seems to stand still in this 150 year-old inn.

The tranquility found in a cup of freshly-brewed tea is what draws new friends to our tea room from all over the country. Nearly everyone who visits has spent one to three hours on their pilgrimage to the inn. They sometimes linger an extra hour in the garden or on the riverbank before returning to the world. Enchantment is a difficult state of mind to leave behind.

Tea and the love of all that is beautiful are the common elements which bring our guests together. Beauty at its simple best is in the communal cup which countless generations have held in their hands. It urges us to pause, drink deeply, and savor all that is right about the world.

Winter, by Irina Ilina

WINTER

December - Angelic Tea
January - Fireside Tea
February - Tea for Lovers

An Angelic Tea

Featured Tea: Harney & Sons Cinnamon Tea
Orange Tea Bread
Christmas Ribbon Sandwiches
Angel Biscuits with Country Ham Spread
Angels on Horseback
Cranberry Scones with Orange Date Spread
Angel Sugar Cookies
White Fruit Cake

There are well over 100 images of angels scattered throughout Elmwood Inn. Small porcelain angels found in Vienna, wooden angel bands from Bavaria, antique bisque bud vases with reclining angels, kissing angels - all make up our menagerie which we have collected over the years. Lately though, it is paintings of angels which have made their way into our collection. Our favorite is an angelic watercolor by Irina Ilina, hanging prominently at the foot of the staircase.

The word "angel" come from the Greek word *angelos*, meaning messenger. Angels appear in classical myth and philosophy, in the vision of Shamans, in Hinduism, Buddhism, Taoism, Zoroastrianism, and Islam, as well as Judaism and Christianity. In all traditions, angels serve as messengers of God and are said to hover between heaven and earth.

It only makes sense that people who enjoy the quiet solitude and gentle spirit which accompanies the celebration of tea should also appreciate the peace which an angel - artistic or otherwise - brings to a home. With that spirit in mind, we have collected a heavenly feast of Christmas tea time recipes based on the theme of angels. From Southern United States Angel Biscuits to English Angels on Horseback, you will find something to please the palate of all your Christmas guests. The meal is complete with Harney & Sons delicious Hot Cinnamon Spice Tea, a blend of black teas, three types of cinnamon, orange peel, and sweet cloves.

Deciding on which Christmas recording to recommend was a difficult task. We finally agreed on a group we have twice heard in person. Chanticleer is the only full-time classical vocal ensemble in the United States. Named for the "clear-singing" rooster in Chaucer's *Canterbury Tales*, this a cappella men's group was founded in San Francisco in 1978. Their uniquely pure sound and seamless blend have earned the group its reputation as "an orchestra of voices" who thrill audiences worldwide with their 100 annual performances. Music is well said to be the speech of angels. You will find within the songs of this ensemble a calming voice which - as an angel should - gives us a glimpse of the divine.

Recommended recording: Chanticleer/*Sing We Christmas*
Teldec Classics International 4509-94563-2

Orange Tea Bread

This tea bread can be made ahead of time and kept frozen until a few hours before your guests arrive. You may serve it with marmalade for extra flavor.

rind of 4 oranges
2 cups sugar
1 tablespoon butter
2 eggs
4 1/2 cups sifted all-purpose flour
1 teaspoon salt
4 1/2 teaspoons baking powder
1 1/2 cups milk

In a small saucepan, cover the grated rinds with water and par boil for 10 minutes. Drain. Repeat. Drain and add 1 cup sugar with 1/2 cup water. Boil carefully for 20 minutes. Remove from heat and add butter. Let cool.

Preheat oven to 350 degrees F. Mix eggs and remaining cup of sugar. Add cooled rind. Alternate adding sifted flour, salt, and baking powder with milk to orange mixture. Pour into a greased loaf pan and bake for 45 minutes. Sprinkle sugar over the top and decorate with curled orange rind.

Christmas Ribbon Sandwiches

Here's a great way to get your family to eat their vegetables during the winter. This delicious sandwich is a great blending of flavors in a colorful arrangement.

1 package chopped spinach, cooked and drained
4 pieces crispy cooked bacon, chopped
3 tablespoons mayonnaise
salt and pepper to taste
3-4 Roma tomatoes, sliced very thin
white bread

Cook spinach according to package directions. Drain by wringing it in a tea towel. Combine spinach, bacon, and mayonnaise. Season to taste.

To assemble sandwiches, spread the spinach mixture on a slice of white bread. Top with a second slice of bread. Add sliced tomatoes and then top with a third slice of bread. Trim crusts and cut into 3 rectangles. Makes 36 small sandwiches.

Angels on Horseback

This is a delicious, traditional English savory dish recommended by English tea author and friend, Jane Pettigrew. Every tea shop owner in Great Britain owns at least one of Jane's cookbooks.

1 dozen oysters
2 large lemons
6 slices of bacon
cayenne pepper
fresh ground black pepper
toast points
parsley

To make toast points: trim the crusts from white bread, cut each slice into 2 triangles, dredge in melted butter, and lightly toast in the oven at about 250 degrees F.

Juice 2 large lemons. Dip each oyster in lemon juice and sprinkle with cayenne and black pepper. Cut the bacon slices lengthwise. Wrap a piece of bacon around each oyster and place on a baking sheet. A cocktail stick may be needed to hold the bacon in place. Place the baking sheet under a broiler and cook until the bacon is crisp. Do not over cook because the oysters may become tough.

Prepare a serving platter with fresh red leaf lettuce leaves. Lay the cooked oyster on toast points and arrange on the platter. Sprinkle with chopped parsley and use cocktail sticks for serving. Serve while warm.

Angel Biscuits

No one can seem to get enough of these light little biscuits. The dough can be made ahead of time and kept in the refrigerator for one week.

2 3/4 cups all-purpose flour
1 1/2 teaspoons baking powder
1/2 teaspoon soda
1 teaspoon salt
2 tablespoons sugar
1 1/4 teaspoons yeast, dissolved in 2 tablespoons warm water
1/2 cup shortening
1 cup buttermilk, room temperature

Preheat oven to 450 degrees F. In a large bowl, sift together the dry ingredients. Cut in shortening.

In a separate bowl, combine dissolved yeast and buttermilk. Add the buttermilk mixture to the dry ingredients until a dough is formed. On a floured surface, roll out the dough to a thickness of 1/2 inch. Cut into small rounds. Place on a lightly greased baking sheet and bake for 12 to 14 minutes or until lightly browned. Remove from oven, cool slightly, and serve with country ham spread.

Country Ham Spread

Use a good quality Kentucky country ham or a Smithfield ham for this spread. It makes a great picnic sandwich.

1/4 pound thinly sliced country ham
2 tablespoons mayonnaise
1 tablespoon dijon mustard

Chop the ham in a food processor and pour into a small bowl. Add mayonnaise and mustard. Stir until well blended. Place a spoonful of the mixture in the center of an angel biscuit and serve.

Cranberry Scones

You must have cranberries at Christmas and what better way to enjoy them than in a sweet warm scone!

2 cups all-purpose flour
2 teaspoons baking powder
1/2 teaspoon salt
1 stick butter
1/4 cup sugar
1/2 cup fresh or dried cranberries
1/2 cup chopped pecans
2 eggs
2 tablespoons orange juice
1 tablespoon vanilla extract
1 egg white mixed with 1 teaspoon water

Preheat oven to 400 degrees F. Lightly grease a 10-inch circle in the center of a baking sheet.

In a large mixing bowl, stir together flour, baking powder, sugar, and salt. Cut in the butter with a pastry blender until mixture resembles coarse crumbs. Add cranberries and pecans, tossing to coat. In a small bowl, whisk together the eggs, juice, and vanilla. Add flour mixture, stirring quickly to combine. The dough will be slightly sticky. Turn out onto the prepared baking sheet. Pat out into 9-inch circle.

Brush top and sides with egg white. Score the dough with a knife into 8 equal wedges. Bake for 25 minutes or until golden brown. Cool for 5 minutes, then remove with a spatula and transfer to a wire rack. Cut into wedges and serve warm with orange date spread, butter, or cranberry curd.

Orange Date Spread

This versatile spread can be used on scones, tea breads, biscuits, or muffins.

1 8-ounce package cream cheese, room temperature
1 stick butter, room temperature
1/4 cup orange marmalade
1/4 cup chopped dates

In a medium mixing bowl, cream the cheese and butter together until fluffy. Mix in marmalade and dates. Refrigerate until ready to serve.

Angel Sugar Cookies

Use a large angel-shaped cookie cutter to cut out these heavenly creations. Pick up several tubes of cake decorations at the grocery and let the children help in designing their favorite angels.

1 cup butter
2 cups sugar
3 eggs
1/2 teaspoon grated lemon rind
1/4 teaspoon nutmeg
3/4 teaspoon cream of tartar
1 teaspoon salt
4 cups all-purpose flour

Cream together butter and sugar. Add eggs and beat well. Add lemon rind and nutmeg. Mix in flour, cream of tartar, and salt. Chill for at least 30 minutes.

Preheat oven to 400 degrees F. Roll out on a floured board and cut with an angel cookie cutter. Sprinkle with sugar and bake for 10 minutes or until the edges begin to brown. You may decorate with colored icings or sparkling cake decorations if desired. Makes 5 dozen cookies.

White Fruit Cake

This light moist fruitcake should be made several weeks in advance and allowed to soak slowly in brandy while aging. It was made to be accompanied by a cup of hot tea.

2 1/2 cups chopped almonds
2 1/4 cups chopped hazelnuts
2/3 cup diced candied orange peel
2/3 cups diced candied pineapple
2/3 cups candied citron
1 1/2 cups golden raisins
1/2 cup all-purpose flour
3/4 cup milk
1/4 cup brandy
1 teaspoon almond extract
1 1/2 cups unsalted butter, room temperature
2 cups sugar
6 egg yolks
3 1/2 cups all-purpose flour
6 egg whites
1 teaspoon cream of tartar

In a large bowl, combine nuts, fruit, and raisins. Toss with 1/2 cup flour to coat. Set aside. Preheat oven 275 degrees F. Grease and flour a 9-inch tube pan. Line the bottom with wax paper. Grease the wax paper as well. Combine milk, brandy, and almond extract in a small bowl. In a large bowl, beat butter until creamy. Gradually add sugar until batter is light and fluffy. Add egg yolks, one at a time, beating well after each addition. Alternate adding the remaining flour and the milk mixture. Slowly fold in fruit/nut mixture until blended well.

Beat egg whites at high speed until foamy. Add cream of tartar and beat until stiff peaks form. Fold egg whites into batter. Spoon batter into pan. Bake for 1 3/4 hours or until cake tester inserted into center comes out clean. Cool in pan for at least 30 minutes.

Remove from pan and place on rack to continue cooling. Wrap the cooled cake in a cheese-cloth soaked in brandy. Wrap with foil and store in the refrigerator for 2 to 3 weeks, brushing occasionally with more brandy.

<u>Icing ingredients</u>
1 1/2 cups unsifted confectioners' sugar
2-3 tablespoons half and half
1 teaspoon almond extract

On the day of serving, place the cake on a beautiful plate. In a small bowl, combine sugar, cream, and almond extract. Beat until smooth. Spread on top of cake while allowing the icing to run down the sides. Decorate with cherry halves, nuts, and other candied fruit.

January Fireside Tea

Featured Tea: Elmwood Inn Lapsang Souchong

Winter Ambrosia

Spiced Pecans

Welsh Rarebit

Drop Scones

Jam Cake

Surely every one is aware of the divine pleasures which attend a wintry fireside: candles at four o'clock, warm hearthrugs, tea, a fair tea-maker, shutters closed, curtains flowing in ample draperies to the floor, whilst the wind and rain are raging audibly without.

-Thomas De Quincey

January is a quiet month here at the inn. We close our doors to guests while we rest from the busy holiday season and begin planning new recipes and events for the upcoming year. The library often becomes our evening refuge as we sit by the fire and catch up on reading all the books we have collected throughout the year which, until now, we have been too busy to enjoy. The old house braces against the winter winds and we wonder how the first tenants, John and Louisiana Burton, along with their five children, kept warm with only fireplaces to fend off the cold winters of the 1840's. Hot tea and a cozy fire often helps us fight the battle.

Our Fireside Tea could be either an afternoon tea or a high tea. The inclusion of "Welsh Rarebit" certainly qualifies this menu as a hearty meal. For something simpler, combine the jam cake with a dish of ambrosia, accompanied by a large pot of steaming tea.

The recommended tea this month is a smoky Lapsang Souchong, a favorite of tea connoisseurs worldwide. This black China tea is actually smoked-dried over a bed of pine needles. Tradition has it that as Chinese coolies brought the tea to market on their backs, the smoke from their nightly campfires would permeate the heavy packs of tea. The wood-burning aroma was then released when the consumer added boiling water to the withered leaf. Interestingly, this tea was the most requested by British actress Lynn Redgrave when she spent the weekend with us in 1995. Try it with lemon and no milk.

Our musical selection for January is Samuel Barber's *Adagio for Strings*. It has, for years, been the most frequently performed concert work by an American composer. The composition begins quietly with a feeling of subdued but deep sadness, builds to a climax of extreme poignancy, and slowly returns to the simple, melancholy mood of its opening. Its use in movies has made it a familiar theme to even non-concertgoers.

A glowing fire, hot tea, good books, quiet music and gentle friends...Lucky you!!

Winter Ambrosia

"Food for the gods" is certainly the correct title for this traditional fruit medley. Find a tall glass compote at your local antique market to display the colorful ingredients.

3-4 large seedless navel oranges
2 large pink grapefruits
1/2 fresh pineapple, cored
3 1/2 ounces flaked coconut
1/2 cup fresh raspberries
1/4 cup *Chambord*

Peel the oranges and grapefruit. Remove the seeds and any membrane from the sections. Cut sections into 1/8-inch slices. Cut pineapple into bitesize chunks before adding to the citrus fruits. Place in a glass compote. Pour the *Chambord* over the top and turn the fruit a couple of times in order to distribute the liqueur. Sprinkle with coconut and top with fresh raspberries. Serve in clear goblets.

Frosted Pecans

Gourmet catalogs are full of advertisements for premium coated nuts these days. This easy recipe will allow you to make your own gourmet snack food at a fraction of the retail cost.

1/2 cup butter
2 egg whites
1 cup brown sugar
1 pound whole pecans
Creole seasoning or seasoned salt

Melt butter in a 9x13 pan in a 300 degree F. oven. Meanwhile, beat egg whites until very stiff. Gradually add brown sugar until mixture is thick and smooth. Fold in pecans until all are coated with the egg white mixture.

Drop by spoonfuls into melted butter and bake. After 10 minutes, turn the pecans and sprinkle with Creole seasoning. Continue to turn and separate every 10 minutes for 1 hour or until brown. Cool in the pan.

Drop Scones

About the only place you still find drop scones today is in the rural tearooms of Scotland. We found them outside of St. Andrews at Kind Kyttocks Tearoom in the village of Falkland. They look like small pancakes. You will probably find them served cold. We prefer them fresh off the griddle.

1 3/4 cup self-rising flour
2 1/2 tablespoons sugar
1 teaspoon cream of tartar
2 eggs
1 cup milk

Sift together flour, sugar, and cream of tartar. In another bowl, whisk together eggs and milk. Pour into flour mixture and combine quickly, making a thick batter.

Oil and preheat a griddle over medium heat. Drop heaping tablespoons of batter on the hot griddle. Cook until batter bubbles completely. Carefully turn and cook until golden brown. Place on a wire rack and keep warm until all scones are done. Serve warm with fresh fruit, honey butter, fruit curd, marmalade, or preserves.

Recommended Recording: Samuel Barber/*Adagio for Strings*
Saint Louis Symphony Orchestra/Leonard Slatkin, EMI CDC 49463

Welsh Rarebit

The argument continues as to whether this dish is called "rarebit" or "rabbit". The story goes that a poor Welshman's rabbit was only a piece of toast under cheese sauce. Someone must have pointed out that the dish was no rabbit, but it was a rare bit. Thus, a new word was born.

1 loaf bakery white bread, unsliced
3/4 cup all-purpose flour
2 teaspoons salt
2 teaspoons dry mustard
1 teaspoon paprika
dash of hot paprika or cayenne pepper
3/4 cup cold milk
2 eggs, beaten
2 tablespoons butter
1 1//4 pounds very sharp cheddar cheese, grated
3 cups hot milk
1/2 cup beer, room temperature
parsley

Preheat oven to 250 degrees F. Slice bread into 3/4-inch slices. Place on a cookie sheet and bake for 45 minutes. Using a double boiler, blend together flour, salt, mustard, and paprika. Add cold milk, eggs, and butter. Whisk constantly and cook until mixture is smooth and slightly thickened. Add cheese and stir until melted. Add hot milk. Cook until thick. Just before serving, stir in beer.

Place 2 slices of toasted bread on a plate and top with cheese sauce. Garnish with parsley and serve while hot.

Caramel Bourbon Sauce

Elmwood Inn was known years ago for its outstanding Bourbon Sauce. Here is our recipe for a Caramel Bourbon Sauce to use over cakes or ice-cream. Store it in the refrigerator and warm it up for a last-minute dessert.

1/4 cup butter
1/4 cup brown sugar
1/2 cup half and half
2 cups sifted confectioners' sugar
2 tablespoons Bourbon
dash of salt

Melt butter in a saucepan over medium heat. Add brown sugar and half and half. Stir until sugar is dissolved. Beat in the confectioners' sugar, Bourbon, and salt. Bring to a boil for 1 minute. Remove from heat. Spoon over slices of jam cake or ice-cream.

Jam Cake

Jam cakes make a wonderful alternative to the traditional holiday fruit cake. The aroma of spices mingles with the lingering smell of fine Kentucky Bourbon to make a moist dessert your family will look forward to year after year.

1 cup butter, melted
6 eggs, beaten
4 tablespoons buttermilk
2 cups brown sugar
1 cup blackberry jam
1 cup crushed pineapple, drained
3 cups all-purpose flour
1 teaspoon soda
2 tablespoons cocoa
2 teaspoons cinnamon
2 teaspoons allspice
2 teaspoons nutmeg
1 cup walnuts (chopped)
1/2 cup flaked coconut
1 cup raisins
1/4 cup Bourbon

Preheat oven to 325 degrees F. Grease and flour a 9-inch tubepan. Mix eggs, melted butter, buttermilk, brown sugar, blackberry jam, and crushed pineapple together.

In a separate bowl, sift flour with soda, cocoa, cinnamon, allspice, and nutmeg. Stir in walnuts, coconut, and raisins.

Slowly add the dry mixture to the wet mixture. Mix well. Pour into prepared tube pan and bake 1 1/2 hours or until a tester comes out clean. Cool in pan for 30 minutes, then turn out onto a cake rack to cool completely. Wrap the cake in a cheesecloth soaked with a premium Kentucky Bourbon. Wrap in aluminum foil and store in a cake tin. Brush with Bourbon once each week until ready to serve.

February Tea for Lovers

Featured Tea: Lasko's Courtship Tea
Frosted Fruit
White Chocolate Muffins
Lobster Newberg in Puff Pastry
Shrimp in Canoes
Chocolate Tea Bread with Orange Cream
Chocolate Valentine Cake
Pink Champagne Granita

Fresh flowers, Chopin playing in the background, beautiful food, a painting of Romeo and Juliet contemplating their fate, a romatic tea blended for a romantic occasion ...all these elements combine to make an irresistible setting for Cupid to work his charms.

Valentine season is becoming a tradition at Elmwood Inn and bookings for tea fill quickly. Young couples, old couples, hoping-to-be couples all take part in the relaxing tea ceremony where two people may concentrate on each other away from the distractions of everyday life. Wives, often married for 25 years, have told us that they had more pleasant conversation with their husbands during our hour-long tea than in a month of married life.

Several years ago, we found a box of turn-of-the-century Valentines at an estate auction. The collection of lovingly-kept German-made keepsakes had been shared between two ladies in Cincinnati. Each embossed card had a short note written on the back. Several of the delicate designs were made to open up like butterflies or three-dimensional garden scenes. We like to share these antique collectables with our guests by placing them on the mantle for all to enjoy.

Our featured blend for February is called *Courtship Tea*, designed by Donna and Ron Lasko of Massachusetts. This talented couple has developed a unique lecture series featuring tea traditions from the Victorian and Edwardian eras. Their re-creations of turn- of-the-century romanticism has received wide recognition all over New England. Donna personally endorses her unique tea blend as a "romance enhancer."

What better choice of music could accompany this scene than that of Frederic Chopin? His music is a distinctive blending of romantic and classical elements. Passionate and impetuous, his keyboard writing encompasses a wealth of coloristic and dynamic variety. Pay close attention to *Prelude in D flat Major*, opus 28 "Raindrop". Chopin completed this work at the height of a stormy love affair with the lady novelist George Sand. The couple shared a home on the island of Majorca in the winter of 1839. While there, Chopin had a relapse of tuberculosis and the two were quarantined in an abandoned Carthusian monastery, complete with a suite overlooking the gardens. He put his confinement to good use by composing 24 short preludes.

Recommended recording: Chopin/*Favorite Piano Works*
Vladimir Ashkenazy, Artist, London 444 830-2 (2 CD Set)

Frosted Fruit

Fruit, presented in this fashion, becomes a work of art. Frosted and cascading out of a tall glass compote, it serves as the centerpiece for our romantic tea time scene.

several small bunches of red and green grapes
strawberries
apples
pears
plums
cherries
1 egg white
1-2 cups superfine sugar

Fruit should be washed and free from blemishes. Beat the egg white well. Brush onto fruit with a pastry brush. Leave for a moment, but not until dried. Sprinkle heavily with sugar on all sides, letting excess sugar fall off. Place on a tray lined with wax paper to dry. Arrange in a glass compote, fruit bowl, or stand.

White Chocolate Pecan Muffins

White chocolate is finding its way into more and more recipes these days. The white flakes of chocolate mingled with the pecan pieces will pleasantly surprise your guests.

1/4 cup melted butter, cooled
1 egg
1/2 cup orange juice concentrate
1/2 cup milk
2 cups all-purpose flour
1/4 cup sugar
1 tablespoon baking powder
1/3 cup white chocolate, grated
1/4 cup chopped pecans

Preheat oven to 375 degrees F. Lightly spray 3 mini muffin tins with cooking spray. In a medium bowl, combine butter, egg, orange juice concentrate, and milk. Blend and set aside.

In a large bowl, combine flour, sugar, baking powder, white chocolate, and pecans. Mix together. Make a well in the center of the dry ingredients. Pour in the milk mixture and stir until just moistened. Do not overmix. Fill each muffin cup 3/4 full. Bake for 7 minutes or until the tops are light golden brown. Serve warm. Makes 36 mini muffins.

Chocolate Tea Bread

Too often, tea breads are dry and predictable. This recipe includes cocoa, coffee, dates, and walnuts to give it a festive flavor.

1/2 stick butter, softened
3/4 cup sugar
1 egg
1 tablespoon strong coffee
1/3 cup unsweetened Dutch processed cocoa
1 3/4 cup sifted flour
1 teaspoon baking soda
1/2 teaspoon salt
1 cup chopped walnuts
1 cup chopped dates
1 cup buttermilk

Grease 2 9x5x3 loaf pans and dust with finely crushed bread crumbs. Set aside. Sift together flour, baking soda, and salt. Set aside Preheat oven to 350 degrees F.

In a bowl, cream butter and sugar. Add egg. Reduce mixing speed to "low". Add coffee and cocoa. Add dry ingredients in 3 additions. Add buttermilk in 2 additions. Stir in dates and nuts. Turn into prepared pans and smooth the batter.

Bake for 1 hour or until done. Cool in the pan for 10 minutes. Remove the cake to a rack and continue to cool. Refrigerate the loaf before slicing to prevent crumbling.

Orange Cream Cheese Spread

This versatile spread was made to accompany our Chocolate Tea Bread. However, it can be used on scones, muffins, or even toast for a breakfast delight.

8 ounces softened cream cheese
1/4 cup grated orange rind
juice of 1 orange
3 tablespoons sugar

Using a mixer, combine all ingredients and spread on thin slices of chocolate tea bread.

Chocolate Valentine Cake

If your favorite friend is a chocolate lover, then this cake is the way to his/her heart. What an indulgence - chocolate cake with chocolate glaze, topped with leaves of chocolate.

1/3 cup shortening
1 cup sugar
1 egg, room temperature
1 1/2 cups flour
1 teaspoon baking soda
1/2 teaspoon salt
1/2 cup unsweetened Dutch processed cocoa
1 cup buttermilk
1 teaspoon vanilla

Preheat oven to 350 degrees F. Grease and line with wax paper an 8" or 9" heart-shaped cake pan.

Cream shortening and sugar. Add egg. Sift dry ingredients and add alternately with buttermilk. Stir until just mixed. Add vanilla. Pour batter into pan and bake 30 minutes. Cool on a rack. Frost with a chocolate glaze or your favorite chocolate frosting.

<u>Frosting ingredients</u>
4 1-ounce semi-sweet chocolate
1 ounce unsweetened chocolate
1/2 cup sugar
1/4 cup light corn syrup
1/4 cup cream
4 teaspoons unsalted butter
1 teaspoon vanilla

Over slow heat, melt both chocolates. Add sugar and corn syrup while stirring vigorously. Add cream and cook until smooth and satiny. Add butter slowly. Stir in vanilla.

Place the cake on a rack and cover with the warm chocolate glaze. Decorate with live rose buds or chocolate leaves.

Lobster Newburg

Valentine foods should always be out-of-the-ordinary and flavored with a generous dash of extravagance. This easy recipe serves six for tea or two for dinner.

4 tablespoons butter
4 tablespoons flour
2 cups cream
1 tablespoon sweet paprika
1 teaspoon salt
1 teaspoon dry mustard
1/4 teaspoon white pepper
dash of cayenne pepper
dash of Worcestershire sauce
4 tablespoons dry sherry
3 small lobster tails, cooked, shelled and cut into pieces
baked pastry shells or puff pastry

Melt butter and gradually whisk in flour. Cook slowly for 2 minutes. Gradually add cream, whisking constantly until smooth. Cook 2 more minutes. Add paprika, salt, mustard, and white pepper. Add cayenne pepper and worcestershire sauce. Add Sherry and cook for 2 minutes. Fold in lobster pieces. When lobster is hot, serve over baked puff pastry or in a baked pastry shell.

Pink Champagne Granita

Champagne was never more refreshing than in this icy mix enhanced with a raspberry liqueur. The only problem is what to do with the left over half bottle of champagne!

1/2 bottle champagne
1/2 cup simple syrup
1/4 cup raspberry liqueur

(Use the simple syrup recipe found in the Basics section of this book.) Mix all ingredients together with a whisk or blend together in a blender. Pour into a glass bowl and place in freezer. Stir once every hour for about 3 hours, then when enough ice has formed, leave the mixture to freeze thoroughly. After 6 hours, the granita is ready to scoop into sherbet glasses. Garnish with fresh raspberries.

Shrimp Boats

The Owl and the Pussy Cat went to sea in a beautiful pea-green boat. Edward Lear's poem was the inspiration for this beautiful and delicious nautical creation.

1 pound extra large shrimp, peeled (20-25)
5 green onions, chopped
1/2 cup safflower oil
1/2 cup soy sauce
1 teaspoon ginger
3 cloves garlic
1/2 cup lime juice
1/4 cup molasses or dark brown sugar

Combine all ingredients and marinate in the refrigerator for 3 to 4 hours. Remove the shrimp, skewer and grill 3 minutes on each side. (You may broil in the oven for 5 minutes on each side.) Refrigerate until ready to assemble boats.

Ingredients
20-25 snow peas
1 bunch chives

Wash the snow peas and pat dry. Open the inner side of the pea pod like an envelope. Slide the shrimp into the middle so that the head and tail are protruding from the pod. Lash the shrimp mariner into the pod boat with a long piece of chive and tie securely. Refrigerate 'til ready to serve.

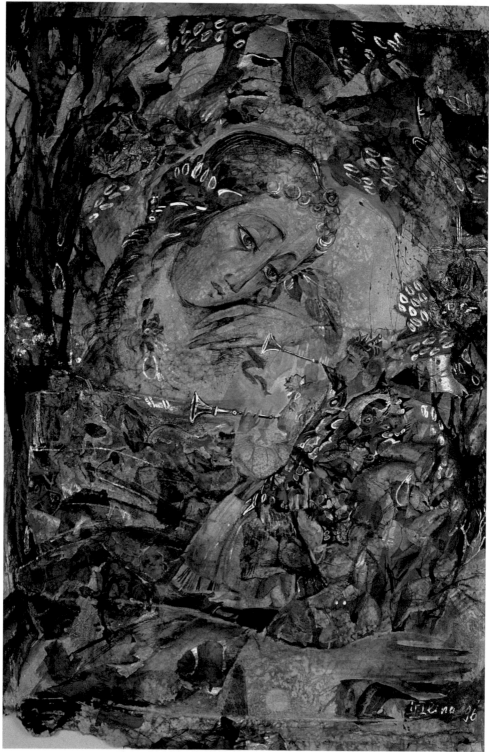

Spring, by Irina Ilina

SPRING

March - Irish Tea

April - Tea with Shakespeare

May - May Day Tea

Irish High Tea

Featured tea: Elmwood Inn Irish Blend
Potato Soup
Irish Soda Bread
Fresh Herb Savory
Smoked Salmon Tea Sandwiches
Beef in a Biscuit
Chocolate Irish Cream Cake
Blackberry Sorbet

Ireland's love of tea has no equal as her citizens boast the highest rate of tea consumption in Europe. Some estimates show that the average resident drinks between four and five cups of tea per day!

Our Irish high tea is a full meal, complete with hot soup and a hearty loaf of country bread fresh from the oven. High tea has traditionally been known as a decent filling meal served with a pot of tea at a dining table after 5:30. The term "high" has nothing to do with elegance. (Afternoon tea is almost always more elegant than high tea.) "High" refers to the height of the table; as opposed to "low" tables where afternoon tea was usually taken. In our region of the United States high tea is comparable to a full supper; the only difference being that the tea is served over ice.

The featured tea with this menu is an Irish blend of teas from Kenya and India. This full-bodied tea holds up well when matched with a variety of foods. Add milk if you wish.

There is no lack of outstanding Irish folk music these days - both live and recorded. The popularity of such groups as the Chieftains has come a long way in reacquainting Americans with music which helped shape the traditional melodies of our nearby Appalachia Mountains region. Pipes, fiddles, dulcimers, and harps all combine for a style of music which can be sometimes haunting, yet always captivating. Our recommended recording is of a lone Celtic harp - a soothing accompaniment to the end of a long day of work.

One of our favorite March teas at Elmwood Inn featured the portrait art of our friend, Wilma Brown. Wilma's paintings of Danville families filled the inn and created considerable interest among our local guests who often knew the subjects of her works. She discovered her artistic talents late in life and, not too many years ago, left her school librarian position in order to devote her life to her newly-discovered vocation. Much to our delight, one of her earliest commissions was a 1990 watercolor of Elmwood Inn. This treasured gift from long-time friends hangs prominently in our hallway.

Recommended recording: *Wind Shadows*
Kim Robertson/Celtic Harp, Invincible Production INVCD111

Potato Soup

What a comforting soup this is on those often cold dark days of March. Made from a good homemade chicken stock, it serves as the centerpiece for a bountiful high tea.

6 medium potatoes
1 large onion (chopped)
3 cups chicken stock
3 cups milk
1 tablespoon butter
chopped parsley
salt
white pepper

Make the stock ahead of time by boiling a chicken carcass with a few root vegetables, onions, and herbs you may have available. Simmer for at least one hour. The stock should then be strained, cooled, and the fat removed from the surface.

Peel and dice potatoes. Chop onion. In a covered soup kettle, melt butter over medium heat. Add onions and potatoes. Gently cook until soft. Pour in stock and milk. Season with salt and pepper to taste. Cover and continue cooking at low heat for about 45 minutes. For a thicker soup, mash some of the potatoes in the pot. Ladle into bowls and top with parsley. Serves six to eight.

Irish Soda Bread

This easy-to-make bread can be quickly baked for breakfast or tea, accompanied by preserves, lemon curd, or whipped butter. The crusty loaf looks beautiful nestled in a country basket.

4 1/2 cups all- purpose flour
1 teaspoon salt
1 teaspoon baking soda
1 teaspoon sugar
2 cups buttermilk

Preheat oven to 450 degrees F. Sift dry ingredients into large mixing bowl. Add buttermilk slowly until a soft dough forms. (You may not need to use the full 2 cups of buttermilk.) Place dough ball on breadboard. Knead dough quickly, but lightly. Do not overwork.

Form a round loaf about as thick as a fist. Lightly grease and flour a baking sheet. Place dough on sheet. Cut a cross shape in the top with a floured knife. Bake for 30-45 minutes. The loaf should sound hollow when rapped on the bottom.

Fresh Herb Savory

Most markets now carry fresh herbs even in March. The visual effect of fresh herbs is part of the attraction in this dish; however, you may substitute dried herbs if fresh sprigs are not available.

Pastry
1 1/2 cups all purpose flour
1/2 teaspoon salt
2 tablespoons vegetable shortening
6 tablespoons chilled butter
5-6 tablespoons ice water

Mix together flour and salt. Cut in shortening and butter with a pastry blender until crumbly. Add the ice water and mix with a fork until well- blended. Place dough in refrigerator for about one hour. Preheat oven to 400 degrees F. On a floured board, roll out enough dough to fit a 10-inch tart pan. Lift into pan. Trim the edge. Bake crust for 10-12 minutes. Remove from oven and reduce temperature setting to 350 degrees.

Filling
5 eggs
2 1/2 cups half and half
1 cup sharp cheddar cheese (grated)
1/2 cup fresh chopped herbs: parsley, oregano, basil, chives
salt and pepper to taste

Whisk together eggs with half and half. Add a dash of salt and pepper. Spread grated cheese over the bottom of crust. Slowly add egg mixture and sprinkle herbs over top. Bake 45-50 minutes in 350 degree F. oven.

Smoked Salmon Tea Sandwich

Debbie Wheat's father, Bob Hook of Louisville, brings back wonderful salmon from his regular fishing trips to Alaska. The fresh catch is smoked and canned for him the same day. Debbie's simple recipe makes good use of this Alaskan delicacy.

1 loaf dense bread
1 can smoked salmon
2 tablespoons mayonnaise
1 teaspoon dijon mustard
1 teaspoon lemon juice
salt and pepper
fresh dill

Mix together salmon, mayonnaise, mustard, and lemon juice. Add salt and pepper to taste. Cut out 2-inch round disks of bread. Spread salmon mixture on rounds and top with fresh dill.

Blackberry Sorbet

In Ireland, one may find wild blackberry bushes loaded with berries along the country roads from late August to mid-October, especially if a wet summer has been followed by a dry autumn. How wonderful to enjoy a little taste of autumn in early spring with this refreshing dessert.

3-4 cups blackberries
1 cup simple syrup
2 teaspoons blackberry liqueur (optional)

See the Simple Syrup recipe found in the Basics section of this book. In a medium saucepan, combine blackberries with about 1/4 cup simple syrup. Bring to boil, then reduce heat and simmer two minutes. Remove from heat.

Press the mixture through a sieve to remove the seeds. Add the remaining simple syrup and liqueur to the seedless mixture and mix well. Place the bowl containing the mixture into a freezer for six hours; stir occasionally. The sorbet may then be scooped out and served in short goblets.

Beef in a Biscuit

These half-dollar size biscuits may also be served as appetizers or for picnic lunches.

2 cups all-purpose flour
4 teaspoons baking powder
1/2 teaspoon soda
1/2 teaspoon salt
2 tablespoons course ground mustard
1/4 cup vegetable shortening
1 cup buttermilk

Preheat oven to 450 degrees F. Combine dry ingredients. Cut in shortening and blend with pastry blender until crumbly. Pour in buttermilk and mix quickly until dough just holds together.

On a floured surface, knead the dough lightly for 10 seconds. Roll out to 1/2-inch thickness and cut out biscuits with a small round cutter. Place close together on a slightly greased cookie sheet. Bake for 10 minutes or until lightly browned. Makes 2 dozen biscuits.

<u>Roast Beef Filling</u>
1 small sirloin-tip roast (fully cooked)
horseradish
mayonnaise
salt
pepper

Cut the cooled beef into pieces and chop in food processor at medium speed until coarsely ground. Place in bowl. Mix in mayonnaise and horseradish to make a spread. Add salt and pepper to taste.

Cut each biscuit (room temperature) in half and fill with beef spread.

Chocolate Irish Cream Cake

We have had more requests for this recipe than any other cake we have ever served in the tea room. To be served this luscious creation is truly the "luck of the Irish".

1 cup butter
1 cup sugar
4 eggs
1 cup self-rising flour
1/2 cup hot chocolate mix
1/4 cup unsweetened cocoa
1 teaspoon vanilla
milk
3 tablespoons Irish cream liqueur

Cream together butter and sugar. Add eggs, one at a time, beating well after each addition. Sift flour, hot chocolate mix, and cocoa into butter mixture. Fold in with spatula. Add vanilla and Irish cream. Blend with mixer until just smooth. Add enough milk to make a soft dough (not runny).

Preheat oven to 300 degrees F. Grease and line a 9-inch round cake pan with wax paper. Pour in batter and bake for 60-90 minutes or until top of cake springs back to the touch. Remove from oven and cool for 15 minutes. Place on wire rack and cool completely.

Filling
1/2 cup softened butter
2 cups confectioners sugar
1/2 cups Irish cream liqueur

Beat all ingredients together with mixer at high speed until fluffy. Split cake in half and fill between layers allowing some filling to protrude on the edge.

Icing
6 ounces unsweetened chocolate
6 ounces semi-sweet chocolate
1/2 cup cream

In a medium saucepan, melt both chocolates in cream over low heat. Stir until smooth. If mixture becomes too oily, add more cream and whisk until glossy.

While still warm, spread over top of cake and allow to drizzle down the side. Top with chopped walnuts, pecans, or hazelnuts.

"Family of Capulet" by Irina Ilina

April Afternoon Tea on a Theme by William Shakespeare

<u>ACT I</u>
Featured Tea: Elmwood Inn Keemun
Cheddar Cheese Scones with Ginger Cream
<u>ACT II</u>
Merchant Tea Sandwich
English Garden Sandwich
Much Ado Sandwich
Juliet's Sand Tarts
Cherry Tart
<u>ACT III</u>
Titania's Fairy Cake
<u>ACT IV</u>
Romeo's "Mon Ami"

William Shakespeare never drank tea. It wasn't because he disliked the drink; he had never heard of it! The Dutch did not introduce tea to England until 1637, twenty years after the bard's death. Even then the exotic leaf from China was very rare and quite expensive at an equivalent of one hundred dollars per pound. But surely, if there had been such an indulgence as afternoon tea, Shakespeare would have included the custom in his plays. Can you imagine the Capulets inviting the Montagues over for a "nice cup of tea" in order to work out their little disagreement?

Our tea on a Shakespearean theme contains dishes which capture the flavors of 17th century England, along with images conjured up by the master writer himself. The whole idea came about as a result of our travels to England. We discovered tea pots in Stratford-on-Avon decorated with scenes from three Shakespearean plays —*Hamlet, Romeo and Juliet,* and *Midsummer Night's Dream.* These lovely ceramic creations were later imported for use in the Elmwood tea room.

Russian artist Irina Ilina set the stage with her magnificent interpretations of scenes from *Hamlet* and *Romeo & Juliet*, created especially for our "Tea with William Shakespeare." We once wandered into her studio and found her weeping as she painted with the strains of Prokofiev's ballet *Romeo and Juliet* playing in the background.

The featured tea is a simple, yet classic black China tea, Keemun. First produced in 1875, this flavorful tea takes well to milk. It has long been a favorite breakfast tea.

Recommended recording: Mendelssohn/*Overture and Incidental Music - A Midsummer Night's Dream;* Vienna Philharmonic/Andre' Previn, Philips 420 16102

Cheddar Cheese Scones with Ginger Cream

The aroma of freshly baked scones dotted with melted cheddar cheese is irresistible. Unlike our British friends, we serve our scones warm from the oven.

2 cups self-rising flour
dash of ground red pepper
1 1/2 cups sharp cheddar cheese, shredded
6 tablespoons butter
1/2 cup buttermilk
1 egg
1 egg yolk mixed with water for glaze

Preheat oven to 350 degrees F. In a large bowl, stir together the flour and red pepper. With a pastry blender, cut in butter until mixture resembles coarse crumbs. Add cheese.

In a small bowl, whisk together buttermilk and egg. Add to flour mixture and stir until just combined.

Place dough on floured surface and knead 5-6 times. With a floured rolling pin, roll out dough to a 2-inch thickness. Cut out with a floured biscuit cutter and place on a lightly greased cookie sheet. Brush tops with egg yolk mixture and bake for 15 minutes or until lightly browned. Serve with ginger cream.

Ginger Cream

While we created this spread for scones, it may also be used on biscuits or tea cakes.

1 8-ounce package cream cheese, room temperature
1 1/2 sticks unsalted butter, room temperature
1 1/2 teaspoons ginger
1/2 teaspoon nutmeg
1/4 cup powdered sugar
heavy cream

Combine cream cheese and butter with electric mixer. Add ginger, nutmeg, and sugar. Then add enough cream to make a smooth spread. Refrigerate until ready to serve. Place in small serving dishes so each guest may spread as much as they like on their scones.

Much Ado Sandwich

The sweet taste of cranberries and raspberries melds with a thin slice of meat loaf to make a more-than-ordinary tea sandwich. Served on a biscuit, this unusual sandwich makes a great finger sandwich for receptions.

1 1/2 pounds ground round
1 cup bread crumbs or bread crusts
3/4 cup milk
2 eggs
1/2 cup finely chopped onion
1 teaspoon thyme
1 teaspoon salt
1 teaspoon parsley
pinch ground pepper

Preheat oven to 350 degrees. Combine milk, egg, salt, and pepper. Add bread crumbs or crusts and soak until very soft. Using your hands, add meat, onions, and herbs. Mix well. Form into a loaf and place into a small 3x5 loaf pan. Bake for 70-75 minutes. Remove from pan and allow to cool in the refrigerator.

See the biscuit recipe on page 40 of this book.

Cran-raspberry Sauce

1 bag fresh or frozen whole unsweetened cranberries
1 cup frozen whole unsweetened raspberries
1 1/2 cup sugar
1/4 cup water
1 teaspoon horseradish

Place berries and sugar in saucepan with water. Bring to a boil, stirring constantly. Reduce heat but continue to cook until most of the berries have popped. Mixture should be thick and sticky. Remove from heat and refrigerate.

When cool, add 1 teaspoon horseradish per cup of fruit. To assemble sandwiches: place a thin slice of meat loaf on the bottom half of a biscuit. Top with berry mixture and replace biscuit top.

Cherry Tarts

These small tarts are perfect for serving at a formal tea, garden party, or just for dessert. They also make a marvelous conclusion to an outdoor picnic - no forks necessary.

<u>Crust ingredients</u>
1 cup softened butter
2 cups flour
1 cup sugar

Preheat oven to 350 degrees F. Combine ingredients. Roll on a floured surface until very thin. Cut into rounds using a cookie or biscuit cutter. Carefully fit rounds into 2 small muffin tins. Bake until slightly brown. Cool slightly and then remove with a knife. Allow shaped pastry to cool undisturbed.

<u>Filling ingredients</u>
1 can sour cherries
1/2 cup sugar
2 tablespoons cornstarch
2 tablespoons cherry gelatin

Drain juice from cherries and reserve 1/2 cup liquid. Combine sugar, gelatin, and cornstarch in medium saucepan. Add reserved cherry juice. Cook at a low boil for 3-4 minutes while stirring constantly. Remove from heat for 5 minutes. Add drained cherries. Fill tart shells and chill. Serve with a dot of creme chantilly.

Juliet's Sand Tarts

During the time of the early Christian church, small cakes or cookies were baked to celebrate certain saints' days. They were baked in the shape of a heart and called "Life Cakes". Over the centuries the name became distorted from "saints' hearts" to "sand tarts".

1 cup butter
2 cups sugar
1 teaspoon lemon rind, grated
3 egg whites
3 1/2 cups flour, sifted
1 teaspoon salt
1 teaspoon baking powder
1/4 cup sugar and cinnamon mixture

Cream butter and sugar together. Add grated lemon rind and egg whites and mix well. Sift flour, salt, and baking powder together. Blend with butter mixture and chill well.

Preheat oven to 350 degrees F. Roll dough to 1/8 inch thickness. Cut into heart shapes with cookie cutter. Place on dry cookie sheet and bake for 8 minutes.

Remove from oven and dust with sugar and cinnamon. Return to oven for 2 more minutes. Makes about 5 dozen cookies.

Romeo's "Mon Ami"

What a delight to both the eye and palate! This final act is served in antique green dishes with a freshly picked wild violet adorning the custard. How simple and beautiful.

2 cups heavy cream
1/4 cup plus 3 tablespoons sugar, divided
2 egg yolks
2 tablespoons cornstarch
1 tablespoon peach brandy

Combine milk and 1/4 cup sugar in small saucepan. Heat and stir until sugar dissolves. Do not boil. Remove from heat. Combine egg yolks with 3 tablespoons sugar in a medium bowl. Gradually add cornstarch, whisking well. Slowly stir half of the hot milk mixture into the egg mixture. Add the remaining milk mixture, whisking all the while.

Cook over medium heat, whisking constantly, until mixture is smooth and thickened. Add peach brandy. Pour into bowl and cover with plastic wrap. Chill.

Spoon into small serving dishes and garnish with a small edible flower, such as a violet.

English Garden Sandwich

Don't let the first ingredient of this colorful sandwich fool you. The exotic taste of spiced fruit will make your guests think you have worked culinary magic.

2 boxes frozen chopped spinach (cooked to package directions)
2 tablespoons butter
1/2 cup currants
1/4 cup orange juice
1/2 teaspoon ground cloves
1 teaspoon nutmeg
1/4 cup vinegar
2 tablespoons sugar
salt & pepper to taste
bakery white bread
3 tablespoons melted butter
1 hard-boiled egg, finely chopped
sweet paprika

Soak currants in orange juice for 20 minutes. Cook spinach and completely drain all liquid. Melt 2 tablespoons butter in skillet. Add spinach and lightly sauté. Add currants, cloves, and nutmeg.Stir. Add vinegar and sugar. Add salt and pepper to taste. Continue to cook slowly until liquid evaporates. Remove and chill.

Make toast triangles by removing crust from a good white bread. Dredge in melted butter or margarine and bake on a cookie sheet in a 250 degree F. oven until golden brown. Cool. Spread spinach mixture over toasted triangle and top with chopped egg. Sprinkle with sweet paprika. Makes about 2 dozen sandwiches.

Merchant Tea Sandwich

This hearty chicken salad boasts of a variety of dried fruits combined with chunks of chicken. This symphony of flavors prompted one of our guests to proclaim "My taste buds were singing hymns!"

4 boneless chicken breasts, cooked and chopped into bitesize pieces
2 stalks celery, chopped
1/2 medium onion, minced
1/2 cup chopped pecans or walnuts
1/2 cup chopped dried apricots
1/2 cup golden raisins
1/2 cup chopped prunes
mayonnaise
white bread cut into small rounds

In a large bowl, mix together all chopped ingredients. Add just enough mayonnaise to hold the mixture together. Place a small mound on round pieces of white bread.

Titania's Fairy Cake

Light and delicious, the taste of this cake from Midsummer Night's Dream is so magical, your guests will think it was made by fairies themselves.

1/2 cup vegetable shortening
1/2 cup butter
1/2 cup brown sugar
4 eggs
1/2 cup molasses
1 1/2 cup self-rising flour
1 teaspoon allspice
1 teaspoon ginger
1 teaspoon cinnamon
1/2 teaspoon salt
2 tablespoons milk
1 8-ounce jar Elmwood Inn Lemon Curd

Preheat oven to 300 degrees F. Cream shortening, butter, and brown sugar until fluffy. Add molasses. Add eggs one at a time, blending well after each addition. By hand, fold in flour and spices. Add salt and milk. Beat quickly with mixer until smooth. Pour into 9-inch round pan which has been greased and lined with wax paper.

Bake for 70 minutes or until middle springs back when touched. Cool in pan for 10 minutes. Remove from pan and continue to cool on rack. Split cake in half horizontally and spread Elmwood Inn Lemon Curd over the bottom layer. Replace the top half. Ice with either a simple lemon icing or with sweetened whipped cream decorated with candied ginger.

Afternoon Tea for a Day in May

Featured tea: Jasmine
Spicy Chicken Tea Sandwiches
Bluegrass Asparagus Tea Sandwiches
May Flower Tea Sandwiches
Fresh Spinach Tarts
White Cheddar & Chive Scones with Herb Butter
Double Dipped Chocolate Strawberries
Rhubarb Bars
May Pole Cake

May Pole celebrations have once again come to the lawn of Elmwood Inn. The festive event was surely a tradition when the mansion served as an academy from 1896 until 1924. Now students from the local elementary school parade the short distance through town and across the Chaplin River to our lawn on May Day. Strains of English folk music - along with our chubby beagle, Freckles - greet the excited children as they reach the foot of the walk bridge. They come carrying small baskets of freshly-picked flowers and dressed in their Sunday-best.

The eager children place their bouquets around the base of the pole and unfurl the long colorful streamers to begin welcoming the arrival of longer days and warm breezes. Children and teachers weave their ribbons into fascinating patterns as they dance around the pole much the same way children have celebrated spring for centuries.

The sight of this colorful event, accompanied by nature's own awakening green leaves and yellowing forsythia, is often too good to keep to yourself. We would like to invite everyone to come and see that here, at least at this moment, time has stood still in our historic village. The passing of time is marked only by the movement of ducks gliding by on the peaceful river just a few yards away. All the while, memories are being etched in young minds which will last a lifetime.

All this activity invariably works up an appetite in our revelers. The only thing that could possibly add to the joy of the morning is a celebration of tea. The class has reviewed their manners and now they begin to file up the steps and cross the worn threshold into the inn as countless schoolmates did a century ago. They take their seats in the dining room for a light morning tea before reluctantly making their way back to school. The teachers always comment on how well the class has behaved. Once again, tea has worked its gentle magic.

Kentucky artist, Holly VanMeter brings the vivid colors of a spring garden indoors with her floral watercolors which often grace our walls during the the month of May. Her many Central Kentucky friends look forward to her popular exhibits at the inn.

All this floral activity leads to our featured tea, Jasmine - the world's most popular scented tea. This green China tea is blended with dried jasmine flowers. As with all green teas, be sure to heat your water to no more than 170-185 degrees F.

The lively dances and pastoral quality of Grieg's Peer Gynt have long made this work a orchestral standard with sustaining appeal. You'll recognize "Morning Mood" and "In the Hall of the Mountain King" from movie scores of days gone by.

Recommended recording: Peer Gynt by Edvard Grieg
San Francisco Symphony Orchestra/ Herbert Blomstedt, London 425 448-2

Spicy Chicken Salad Tea Sandwich

This tangy tea sandwich can also be made with full slices of bread and enjoyed at your next country picnic or family reunion. Be ready to share the recipe with your friends.

Tomato Preserves Ingredients:
2 14 1/2-ounce cans diced & peeled tomatoes
2 tablespoons lemon juice
3 cups sugar
1 box pectin, no sugar
1 tablespoon herb seasonings
1 tablespoon Tiger sauce (optional)
1 cup coarsely-chopped pecans (optional)

Mix tomatoes, lemon juice, pectin, and spices in a medium saucepan. Bring to a boil. Stirring constantly, add sugar and boil for 1 minute more. Add pecans and pour in sterilized jars. Keep refrigerated up to 3 weeks.

Chicken Salad Ingredients:
5-6 chicken breasts, cooked, de-boned, diced
1/4 cup chopped green onion
1 cup mayonnaise
1/2 cup chopped walnuts
salt & pepper to taste
whole wheat bread
leaf lettuce

Blend chicken with onion, mayonnaise, walnuts, salt, and pepper. Spread chicken mixture on whole wheat bread slice. Spread spicy tomato jam on separate slice. Assemble the sandwich by placing a leaf of lettuce on the chicken salad, then cover with the tomato jam slice. Trim crusts and cut into two triangles.

May Flower Tea Sandwich

These lovely sandwiches shaped like cala lilies have been known to fool honey bees in search of nectar. The phrase "too beautiful to eat" may be applied here.

1 8-ounce package cream cheese
1/4 cup orange marmalade
1/4 teaspoon almond extract
25 pieces white bread, cut into 2-inch rounds
1 small package slivered almonds
25 large wild violet leaves (washed)
yellow food coloring

Using an electric mixer, mix together the cream cheese, marmalade, and extract until smooth. Flatten each piece of bread with a rolling pin and spread with enough cheese mixture to just cover the bread. Pinch together 1/3 of the round to form an open cone.

Coat almonds with yellow food coloring and place one sliver into the throat of each bread cone. Place the assembled flower on a wild violet leaf and serve.

White Cheddar and Chive Scones

Our big-city guests often suggest that we could make a good living by just selling our scones in a major metropolitan area. This recipe would probably be the number one seller. We could suggest that you eat them while they are warm, but scones never last long enough around our inn to get cold.

2 cups self-rising flour
1/2 cup butter
1/4 cup sharp white cheddar cheese, grated
1/8 cup fresh chopped chives
1/2 cup buttermilk
1 egg

Preheat oven to 350 degrees F. Cut butter into flour and mix with a pastry blender until mixture resembles coarse crumbs. Add cheese and chives. Whisk together egg and buttermilk. Add to flour mixture. Stir enough to combine ingredients loosely.

Pour out onto floured surface and knead 6 or 7 times. Roll out dough to about 1/2 inch thickness. Cut with a round biscuit cutter and place on a lightly greased baking sheet. Bake 15-20 minutes or until light golden brown. Makes 1 dozen scones. Serve warm with herb butter.

Fresh Spinach Tart

Our spring garden overflows with early spinach which has come back to life after lying dormant throughout the cold winter. Plant your crop in early September and you will be treated to two pickings --- fall and spring.

3 eggs, lightly beaten
1 cup half and half
salt & pepper to taste
1/2 cup minced onion
1/2 cup finely-chopped pimento
1 cup shredded Swiss cheese
1 1/2 cups fresh spinach (chopped)
1 9-inch slightly baked tart shell

Preheat oven to 350 degrees F. Line a tart pan or pie pan with pastry crust. (See the pastry recipe in the Basics section.) Bake for 7 minutes. In a large bowl, combine eggs, half and half, seasonings, onions, and pimento. Add cheese and spinach. Pour into tart shell. Bake for 45-50 minutes.

Herb Butter

By late spring our herb garden is ready to yield its bounty. This versatile herb butter makes a wonderful spread for scones, as well as a delicious seasoning for freshly steamed vegetables.

1 cup (two sticks) butter, room temperature
4 ounces cream cheese, room temperature
fresh chopped herbs—oregano, chives, basil, parsley

Mix butter and cream cheese together with an electric mixer until fluffy. Add herbs and mix together quickly. Store in refrigerator until ready to serve.

Double Dipped Strawberries

Children and adults alike enjoy these delicious springtime treats. Many of our guests give into temptation and eat them first.

36 large fresh strawberries
1 1/2 cups semi-sweet chocolate chips
1 tablespoon vegetable shortening
1 1/2 cups chocolate sprinkles

Rinse strawberries and pat dry on paper towels. Line a baking sheet with waxed paper. In the top of a double boiler, melt chocolate and shortening over simmering water until mixture is smooth. Hold individual strawberries by the crown and dip the small end of each berry into chocolate. Do not get chocolate on the crown. Place berries on wax paper. Scatter sprinkles on the berries while chocolate remains wet. Refrigerate at least one hour before serving.

Rhubarb Bars

The tart taste of fresh springtime rhubarb is something many of us can remember from our mother's pies when we were children. We are now introducing a whole new generation to this delicacy.

2 1/2 sticks butter, softened
2 1/2 cups flour
1/2 cup confectioners sugar
1 egg white (reserve yolk for filling)

Preheat oven to 350 degrees F. Lightly grease a 10 x 14 cookie sheet.

Using either a mixer or your hands, blend flour, sugar, and butter. Press dough into cookie sheet. Brush with egg white. Bake until just golden or about 25 minutes. Let cool slightly before filling is added.

Filling ingredients

1 full egg plus yolk from crust ingredients list
1 1/2 cup sugar
5 tablespoons flour
1/4 teaspoon salt
4 cups thinly sliced rhubarb

Mix eggs, sugar, flour, and salt. Add rhubarb and mix gently by hand until all pieces are well-coated. Spread over cooled crust. Bake 45 minutes or until just golden. Cool before cutting.

May Pole Cake

Swirls of red raspberries discovered in each slice of this delicious cake will remind you of long streamers flowing down from a May pole. You may feel like a child again!

"May Flowers" by Holly VanMeter

     2 sticks butter, softened
     3 cups sugar
     6 eggs
     3 cups all-purpose flour
     1 cup sour cream
     1/4 teaspoon soda
     1/2 teaspoon salt
     1 teaspoon vanilla
     1/2 teaspoon lemon flavoring
     1/4 teaspoon orange flavoring
     1/4 teaspoon almond flavoring
     1/4 cup raspberry preserves

Cream butter and sugar; add eggs, one at a time. Add flour alternately with sour cream, beating after each addition. Add soda and salt; beat well and add flavorings.

Preheat oven to 325 degrees F. Pour one-half of batter into a greased tube pan. Warm preserves enough to spread evenly over batter. Add remaining batter. Swirl a knife through the batter a couple of times in order to gently cut in the layer of preserves. Bake for 70 - 80 minutes.

Bluegrass Asparagus Tea Sandwiches

The key to this recipe is to use tender young asparagus shoots before the stalks become too large.

     2 8-ounce packages cream cheese, softened
     2 4-ounce packages blue cheese
     2 tablespoons Worcestershire sauce
     20 small stalks fresh asparagus
     1/4 pound baked ham, sliced thin
     loaf of fresh whole grain bread

Blend first three ingredients using a mixer or food processor. Set aside. Blanch asparagus. Assemble by spreading 1/4-inch blue cheese filling over ham slice. Place four stalks asparagus at the edge of the ham and cheese closest to you. Roll ham, cheese, and asparagus away from you; similar to a jelly roll. When completely rolled, wrap another slice of ham around the roll. Chill. Cut out half-dollar size rounds from the bread slices. To serve, slice the ham roll into 1/4-inch thick rounds and place on small whole wheat bread cut-outs.

Summer, by Irina Ilina

SUMMER

June - Tea in the Rose Garden

July - 1850's Summer Tea

August - Sunflower Tea

Rose Garden Tea

Tea Selection: Elmwood Inn Rose Tea
Country Ham and Tomato Tarts
Apricot and Cheese Tea Sandwiches
Stuffed Nasturtium Leaves
Tomato Aspic with Cucumber
Hazelnut Scones with Rose Petal Conserve
Strawberry Rose Meringues
Chocolate Cake Cookies
Rose Geranium Cake
Strawberry Lemon Mint Sorbet

Tea and roses have a common history which dates back at least two hundred years. The first tea roses arrived in England aboard clipper ships of the East India Company carrying cargoes of teas from China. This is why the name *tea rose* was attributed to these roses, not for their fragrance as was commonly thought. Eventually tea roses were crossed with hybrid perpetuals to produce the famous hybrid tea roses which are the most popular bedding rose today.

No other flower has been so replicated in art. For centuries, rose motifs have been used lavishly in painting, tapestries, and ceramics. Its beauty inspired poetry to heal the spirit; its leaves and hips produced medicines to cure the body, and its petals produced oils to anoint the blessed. Few contemporary artists are able to capture the brilliant way in which light passes through the fragile luminescent petals of the rose as does photographer Carol Henry. Her collection of garden roses serve as the perfect artistic complement to our menu.

The use of rose petals in cooking almost takes on an air of extravagance usually reserved only for those you care most passionately about. Scones with rose conserve, cake laced with rose petals, black China tea blended with roses — it all seems to come from a Jane Austen novel.

Any visitor to Vienna will remember the visions of splendid rose gardens found throughout the city parks, around bandstands, and leading up to the grand palaces. It was in the stimulating environment of this magnificent, cultural-minded city that Wolfgang Amadeus Mozart spent the final ten years of his short, yet prolific, life. Better than most musicians of his day, Mozart knew that the important events of life took place on the battlefield or in the boudoir. So there is a certain appropriateness to the fact that the opening Allegro of *Eine kleine Nachtmusik*, with its fanfares and quick-march brilliance, is followed by a gentle Romance. There is hardly a child today who has not heard the opening motive from this musical gem.

Recommended recording: W. A. Mozart/*Eine Kleine Nachtmusik (A Little Night Music)* Academy of St. Martin-in-the-Fields Chamber Ensemble, Philips 412 269-2

Country Ham and Tomato Tart

A mixing of culinary traditions blends Kentucky country ham with a classic French quiche. These individual tartlets are also wonderful for breakfast or brunch.

6 eggs
3 cups half and half
1/2 teaspoon salt
1/2 teaspoon pepper
1 1/2 cups cheddar cheese, grated
1 cup country ham, thinly sliced and chopped
1 cup Roma tomatoes, thinly sliced
1/4 cup fresh chives, chopped

See the pastry recipe found in the Basics section of this book.

Preheat oven to 350 degrees F. In a large bowl, whisk eggs, half and half, salt, and pepper together. Sprinkle cheese, ham, and tomatoes across the bottom of the partially baked crust. Pour egg mixture over the cheese and sprinkle chives across the top. Bake for 40-45 minutes or until the top is golden brown.

Apricot and Cheese Tea Sandwich

The intense sweetness of dried apricots blended with a full-bodied Stilton cheese makes this tea sandwich a versatile accompaniment for both afternoon teas and receptions.

1/2 cup butter, room temperature
1 tablespoon honey
1 teaspoon balsamic vinegar
1/2 cup walnuts
10 dried apricots
2 cups crumbled Stilton cheese or blue cheese
2 stalks celery
1 1/2 teaspoons fresh thyme
1/8 teaspoon freshly ground pepper
20 slices white bread
1/4 cup mayonnaise
1 cup chopped parsley

In a food processor, chop walnuts, apricots, celery, and thyme. Add butter, honey, vinegar, blue cheese, and pepper. Process until mixture holds together. If more moisture is needed, a little heavy cream may be added until desired consistency is achieved.

Place mixture in a covered container and refrigerate until ready to use. Cut out small rounds from the bread with a 2-inch cookie cutter. Spread each round with the apricot mixture and top with another bread round. Using a small knife, spread a thin layer of mayonnaise around the edge of each sandwich. Then coat the mayonnaise-covered edge with chopped parsley. Place on a holding tray, cover, and refrigerate until time to serve. Makes 20 sandwiches.

Stuffed Nasturtium Leaves

These artistic parcels tied up with chives look as if they came from a Japanese restaurant. Remind your guests that the nasturtiums are edible. The rice-based filling may also be used to stuff tomatoes.

<u>Filling ingredients</u>
4 cups cooked white rice
1 cup diced carrots, blanched
2 cups frozen baby peas, blanched
1/2 cup chopped green onion
1 cup mayonnaise
1 cup *Ojai* lemonnaise
salt and pepper to taste

Combine all ingredients and refrigerate until ready to use.

<u>Wrapping ingredients</u>
30 large nasturtium leaves
30 whole chives

Dip nasturtium leaves in 180 degrees F. water and pat dry. Turn leaves stem side up. Place a small melon scoop portion of rice mixture on each leaf. Pull two sides of the leaf up like a basket. Tie with a single long chive. Clip ends if they are too long.

Tomato Aspic with Cucumber Tea Sandwich

The classic sliced cucumber tea sandwich takes on a new look with the addition of a red tomato aspic heart topped with a tiny dollop of mayonnaise.

5 cups *V-8* vegetable juice
3 3-ounce boxes lemon gelatin
1/2 cup lime juice
dash of Worcestershire sauce
dash hot pepper sauce
30 thin cucumber slices
30 small rounds whole wheat bread

Combine vegetable juice with gelatin and bring to a boil. Stir until dissolved. Remove from heat and add lime juice, Worcestershire, and hot sauce. Pour onto a cookie sheet which has been prepared with either mayonnaise or cooking spray. Refrigerate until firm.

Using a very small heart shaped cookie cutter, cut out small hearts from the congealed aspic. Place a cucumber slice on top of each whole wheat round. Add an aspic heart. Pipe a star of mayonnaise on top and decorate with a tiny piece of dill.

Hazelnut Scones

Scones were originally made in Scotland on a griddle. This slightly crunchy version of our standard scone recipe also makes a great breakfast food.

2 1/2 cups all-purpose flour
1 tablespoon baking powder
1/2 teaspoon salt
1/3 cup packed brown sugar
1 stick butter
1/2 cup chopped hazelnuts
1 teaspoon cardamom
1/2 cup buttermilk
1 egg
2-3 tablespoons cream for glazing

Preheat oven to 400 degrees F. Sift together flour, baking powder, salt, brown sugar, and cardamom. Cut in butter and mix with pastry blender until mixture resembles coarse crumbs. Mix in chopped hazelnuts. Whisk together buttermilk and egg. Pour into flour mixture and mix to form a soft dough. Place dough onto a floured board and roll out to 1/2-inch thickness. Cut into rounds or hearts and place on a lightly greased cookie sheet. Glaze with cream. Bake 12-15 minutes until lightly browned. Make 12 scones.

Rose Petal Conserve

Red roses, such as General McArthur or Etoile de Hollande, make the best conserve and should be gathered when fully open before fading. What a beautiful way to bring the rose garden to the table! Serve with scones.

1 quart rose water
1 package no-sugar pectin
2 cups sugar
5 cups dried rose petals
1/4 teaspoon grated lemon or orange rind

See Rose Water recipe found in the Basics section of this book.

Gather the rose petals and dry away from direct sunlight. Do not use roses from the florist unless you are certain they have been organically grown.

Pour rose water into a 6-quart sauce pan. Gradually add pectin. Whisk constantly for several minutes. Add sugar and boil for 1 minute while stirring constantly. Remove from heat and add dried rose petals and rind. Pour into sterilized jars and adjust tops. Process jars in boiling water bath for 5 minutes. Let cool. Check lids for correct seal.

Strawberry Lemon Mint Sorbet

This refreshing finale is a cross between sorbet and sherbet. It has both an icy consistency and a creamy texture.

6 medium lemons, juiced and strained
2 1/2 cups simple syrup
fresh mint
1/4 cup heavy cream
1/4 cup strawberry puree

Pour 2 1/2 cups cold simple syrup into blender (See Simple Syrup recipe found in the Basics section of this book). Add lemon juice and heavy cream. Blend. 2 or 3 mint leaves may be blended in as well. Pour into a bowl and place in freezer. Stir sorbet every 20 minutes for 2 hours. Add strawberries and swirl throughout. Continue freezing until firm. Scoop portions into serving dishes and garnish with mint.

Strawberry Rose Meringues

Who can resist these cloud-like confections which are so versatile for cradling fruit, whipped cream, or chocolate? They look difficult but are actually easy to make.

4 egg whites
1 cup sugar
dash of salt
1 1/2 cups whipping cream
12 strawberries
6 tablespoons confectioners' sugar
2 tablespoons rose water*

See Rose Water recipe found in the Basics section of this book.

Preheat oven to 250 degrees F. Line cookie sheet with parchment paper. Beat egg whites until soft peaks form. While beating, add salt and very gradually add sugar until granules dissolve. Spoon into pastry bag fitted with a large star tip. Pipe short 2-inch strips of meringue onto prepared cookie sheet and bake for one hour. Meringues should be dry. Cool completely and store in an airtight tin if not using immediately. In a food processor or blender, process 8 strawberries to a puree'. Strain out seeds. Add sugar and rose water to the puree'. Set aside. Whip cream until stiff peaks form. Continue to beat while adding puree'. Using a sharp paring knife, slice the cooled meringues length-wise. Place the strawberry filling between the two half and decorate with a thin slice of strawberry.

"Cottage Rose" by Carol Henry

Chocolate Cake Cookies

Would you like to serve a cake without the bother of cutting individual slices for your guests? These delicious chocolate cookies have the consistency of cake.

1/2 cup butter
1 1/2 cups brown sugar
2 eggs
2 teaspoons vanilla
4 ounces unsweetened chocolate, melted
1 1/2 cups sour cream
3 cups flour
1/4 teaspoons salt
1 1/2 teaspoons soda

Preheat oven to 350 degrees F. Cream butter and sugar. Add eggs and vanilla. Stir in chocolate and sour cream. Add dry ingredients and mix thoroughly. Drop batter by teaspoon on a lightly greased cookie sheet. Bake for 7 minutes. Remove from cookie sheet and ice when cool.

Frosting ingredients
6 tablespoons softened butter
1 pound confectioners' sugar
1 teaspoon vanilla
splash of milk

Cream butter, sugar, and vanilla until fluffy. Add enough milk to make a smooth icing. Spread over the top of each cookie.

Rose Geranium Cake

The magic of this cake is that the geranium leaves make their appearance when the cake is sliced.

1 cup butter, room temperature
2 1/2 cups sugar
6 eggs, beaten
3 cups flour
1/2 teaspoon salt
1/2 teaspoon soda
1 cup sour cream
2 teaspoons vanilla
2 tablespoons rose water
1/4 teaspoons mace
5-6 rose geranium leaves, chopped

See Rose Water recipe found in the Basics section of this book.

Preheat oven to 350 degrees F. Cream butter and sugar until light and fluffy. Add beaten eggs. Blend dry ingredients together and add alternately with sour cream to the egg mixture. Add flavoring and mix well. Fold in chopped rose geranium leaves. Pour batter into prepared tube pan.

Bake for 60-70 minutes or until cake tester comes out clean. Do not over bake. Cool in pan for 1/2 hour, then remove.

Glaze ingredients
1 cup confectioners' sugar
2 tablespoons rose water

Combine ingredients and spread over top of cake. Decorate with fresh rose buds.

An 1850's Summer Tea

Featured Tea: Elmwood Inn Gunpowder Tea
Gingerbread Boys
Lemon Balm Tea Bread
Fried Chicken on Tarragon Biscuits
Chopped Egg and Cress
Prince of Wales Cake

The twenty years leading up to the Civil War — or "The Great Unpleasantry" as it was referred to by many genteel Southern ladies — was a boom time for the Central Kentucky economy. Massive houses sprung up on farms paid for with fine fields of tobacco, corn, and hemp. Herds of cattle, horses, and other livestock, often under the care of slaves, kept the citizenry well-fed and prosperous. Flatboats along the Kentucky and Ohio Rivers kept a steady stream of raw materials heading to the growing eastern markets. Stores, such as the one owned by Elmwood's builder, John Burton, catered to the material needs of families in and around Perrryville.

One of the earliest brick houses built in the community was the Karrick-Parks house, situated on what was the site of the first stockade built by settlers along the Chaplin River in 1783. The present house was built around 1852 by James Karrick. Ten years later it would become a bivouac for Civil War soldiers.

Our 1850's era tea was photographed in the dining room of this historic home. All the foods presented were available at the time. Flour, tea, sugar, salt, ginger, even the curtains were for sale in the Burton General Store just down the street.

Housekeepers of this era would roll up their woolen rugs during the summer months and put down floorcloths which were easier to keep clean and gave the house a cooler atmosphere. Our chef, Debbie Wheat, is known for her colorful floor cloth designs. Her art is displayed on our floors rather than our walls.

What kind of tea did the people of Perryville drink? Probably a green China tea called Gunpowder. Gunpowder has the best keeping quality of any tea made, thanks to its tightly-rolled green leaf. (It does resemble gunpowder.) Because of its long life, it was one of the first green China teas exported for the long clipper ship ride to the Americas. Many frontier experts will tell you that this tea was lighter and easier to store than coffee; making it the drink of choice of most soldiers and frontiersmen.

What kind of music would have accompanied an afternoon tea? It is possible that the songs of Stephen Foster were being sung in the village of Perryville a decade prior to the famous Civil War battle fought here. Foster published his first song, "Open Thy Lattice,

Love", in 1844. (Elmwood Inn was two years old at the time.) American music declared its independence from European tradition with the lyrical melodies of this prolific Pittsburgh song writer. Like Yankee Doodle, he was born on the fourth of July, 1826, the same day that both Thomas Jefferson and John Adams died. It is doubtful that Foster ever visited Kentucky in his short 37 years. But, Kentuckians owe much to this adopted son. His most famous melody, originally based on "Uncle Tom's Cabin", became the official state song—"My Old Kentucky Home".

World class singer Thomas Hampson interprets Foster songs like few other baritones we know. His recording, *American Dreamer*, is captivating for any fan of Foster or of great music. By the way, if the bass you hear in the backup group for "Hard Times, Come Again No More" sounds like Garrison Keillor — it is.

Recommended Recording: *American Dreamer: Songs of Stephen Foster*
Thomas Hampson, baritone, Angel CDC 777 7 546212 8

Gingerbread Boys

Generations of children have taken delight in these boy-shaped cookies decorated with sugar noses and gumdrop eyes. The question is always what to eat first - the head or the feet?

3/4 cup whipping cream
1 1/4 cup dark brown sugar
1/2 cup dark molasses
1 tablespoon baking soda
1 1/2 teaspoon ginger
1 1/2 teaspoon grated orange rind
4 1/2 cups plain flour, sifted

In a large bowl, whip cream until stiff. Fold in dark brown sugar, molasses, baking soda, ginger, and rind. Stir until thoroughly blended. Gradually stir in flour until well blended and smooth. Refrigerate at least 1 hour. When ready to bake, preheat oven to 300 degrees F. Lightly grease cookie sheet. On a floured surface, roll out dough to 1/8 inch thickness. Cut into desired shapes. Place on cookie sheet 1/2 inch apart and bake 10-15 minutes. Remove from sheet and cool.

These little boys can be decorated with raisins before they are baked or painted with royal icing after they are cool.

Fried Chicken in Tarragon Biscuits

Chicken fried in an iron skillet has been a staple of Central Kentucky gatherings for over two hundred years. These delicious morsels may be served warm or cold.

2 pounds boneless chicken breasts, cut into 2-inch pieces
2 cups flour
3 teaspoons paprika
1 teaspoon salt
1 teaspoon ground black pepper
1 teaspoon herb seasonings
1 teaspoon garlic powder
1 teaspoon dried parsley
1/2 teaspoon ground nutmeg
2 eggs
1/2 cup milk
1/2 stick butter
1/4 cup canola oil

Combine the dry ingredients in a large freezer bag and set aside. Beat the eggs in a separate bowl and add milk. Place 1/2 of the chicken pieces in the milk/egg mixture.

Heat a large cast iron skillet over a medium flame. Add the butter and oil. Do not over heat.

Place the wet chicken pieces, 3 at a time, into the flour bag and shake. When the pieces are coated, place them in the hot skillet. Cook for 5 minutes and then turn. Cook 5 more minutes and then remove to a paper towel. Continue this sequence until all pieces have been coated and fried.

See the biscuit recipe found on page 40 of this book.

To assemble, cut the biscuits in half and place a chicken nugget between the two halves. Sandwiches may be refrigerated and then slightly heated before serving.

"19th Century Floor Cloth" by Debbie Wheat.

Prince of Wales Cake

This recipe was adapted from a hand written cookbook compiled by a ladies society of Frankfort, Kentucky around 1850. Only the ingredients were listed with no instructions. Where it calls for coffee cups, use regular measuring cups. Two batters are combined to make one large cake.

7 egg whites, room temperature
2 coffee cups sugar
3 coffee cups plain flour
1 coffee cup sour cream
1 coffee cup butter
1/3 teaspoon soda

Cream butter and sugar until fluffy. Sift flour with soda. Add to butter, alternating with the sour cream. Beat egg whites until soft peaks form and fold into batter. Set aside.

7 egg yolks
1 coffee cup butter
2 coffee cups sugar
1 coffee cup molasses
1 coffee cup sour cream
4 coffee cups flour
1/2 teaspoon soda
2 tablespoons cinnamon
1 teaspoon nutmeg

Preheat oven to 350 degrees F. Cream butter and sugar. Add molasses. Beat in egg yolks. Sift flour with spices and soda. Add to butter mixture, alternating with sour cream. Mix well.

In a large greased and floured tube pan, alternate adding large spoonfuls of batter until all is used. With a knife, swirl one batter into the other. Bake for 1 hour and 20 minutes. Let cool for 15 minutes and remove from pan. Dust with powdered sugar.

Blackberry Tarts

One of the pleasures of owning a farm is the wild blackberry bushes that grow along the fence rows. One must contend with chiggers, Japanese beetles, poison ivy, and the occasional snake in order to gather the harvest, but the effort is always worth it.

4 cups blackberries
1 1/2 cups sugar
3 tablespoons minute Tapioca

Combine ingredients and bring to a slow boil for 5 minutes. Pour into tart or pastry shells.

Lemon Balm Tea Bread

Lemon balm is a common herb found in many kitchen gardens. We often buy our new plants at Shakertown, a restored Shaker Village just minutes away. Early Perryville residents would have used the leaves of this versatile herb as a substitute for fresh lemons.

2 tablespoons fresh lemon balm from herb garden, finely chopped
3/4 cup milk
2 cups all-purpose flour
1 1/2 teaspoons baking powder
1/4 teaspoon salt
6 tablespoons butter, room temperature
1 cup sugar
2 eggs
2 tablespoons lemon zest

Preheat oven to 325 degrees F. Grease a 9x5x3 inch bread pan. Combine chopped lemon balm with milk in a saucepan. Heat, then steep until cool.

In a bowl, mix flour, baking powder, and salt together. Set aside. In another bowl, cream butter and sugar together until light and fluffy. Beat in eggs, one at a time. Add lemon zest. Slowly, add flour mixture to the milk until just blended. Pour batter into prepared pan and bake for 50 minutes. Remove from oven and cool in pan for 10-15 minutes. Turn out onto wire rack. When completely cooled, add glaze.

Glaze ingredients
juice of 2 lemons, strained
2 teaspoons chopped lemon balm
confectioners' sugar

Combine all ingredients to form a thick pourable syrup. Pour over top of cooled bread, letting the excess drizzle over the edge. Decorate with fresh sprigs of lemon balm.

Chopped Egg and Cress Tea Sandwiches

Cress sometimes grows wild in the springs found so abundantly throughout Central Kentucky. This traditional tea sandwich is a common item on English tea trays.

6 hard boiled eggs
3-4 tablespoons homemade mayonnnaise*
salt and pepper to taste
1 bunch fresh water cress
loaf of fresh baked wholegrain bread

*The taste of commercial mayonnaise may be enhanced with the addition of lemon juice and cayenne pepper.

Chop eggs into coarse chunks. Add mayonnaise along with salt and pepper. Mix together quickly. Spread over bread slices, top with watercress and another slice of bread. Cut into four smaller triangles.

Mayonnaise ingredients
2 egg yolks
1 teaspoon salt
2 tablespoons lemon juice
1 cup safflower oil
dash cayenne pepper

In a small bowl, beat egg yolks, salt, and cayenne until thick and lemon colored. Beat in 1/4 cup oil, one drop at a time, until thick. Slowly add 1 tablespoon lemon juice.

Add a steady stream of 1/2 cup oil while beating constantly. Then add the remaining lemon juice and oil while beating. Refrigerate in covered container until ready to use. Makes 1 1/4 cups.

August Sunflower Tea

Featured Tea: Elmwood Inn Earl Grey
Blueberry Bars
Onion Tart
Goldenrod Tea Sandwiches
Sunflower Whole Wheat Scones
Peach Preserves
Summer Cake
Nectarine Sorbet

By late summer, Kentucky vegetable and flower gardens are full of tall stalks of golden sunflowers lifting their brilliant heads to trace the sun's path across a bright blue August sky. In the fifteenth century, Marsilio Ficino recommended that everyone turn toward the mystery of his own nature the way a sunflower turns toward the sun. Even William Blake wrote about the sunflower's strong attraction to its namesake. But it wasn't Europe which gave birth to the sunflower. Ancient caches of seeds have been found in Tennessee dating back to 1500 BC, and history shows that Spanish explorers brought them from the New World over 500 years ago.

Vincent Van Gogh captured the flower in all its splendor in 1888 when he painted a bouquet of sunflowers against an equally golden background. Van Gogh didn't think much of his painting. That didn't keep it from bringing $40 million at auction in 1987.

Young children are often tea time guests at the inn. Sometimes they come dressed in their finest clothes to celebrate a birthday or a holiday. Several of our young friends joined us for a sunflower-inspired tea on the lawn beside the Chaplin River. Much to their delight, families of ducks and geese glided by on the water and were treated to bits of leftover scones by the children.

Our recipes for a Sunflower Afternoon Tea attempt to capture the brilliant colors of this delightful flower. Apricots, nectarines, and pineapples all add their flattering hues to our culinary palette. Three local artists, Irina Ilina, Debbie Wheat, and Holly VanMeter contributed their own sunflower paintings to brighten our tea room for our summer celebration.

The choice of tea to accompany this pleasurable experience is Earl Grey. This tea is blended with oil of bergamot pressed from the rind of a pear-shaped citrus that is grown in the Mediterranean region. Tradition has it that Charles Earl Grey was given the blend while a British diplomat to China in the early 1800's. Earl Grey is, by far, the most popular flavored tea blend in western society today.

The hot slow pace of August calls for music with an unhurried tempo — something relaxing and refreshing. *Parkening Plays Bach* is such a collection. Christopher Parkening is arguably America's greatest guitar virtuoso. His playing of a very technically challenging program of Bach works is both sensitive and intelligent. *Jesu, Joy of Man's Desiring* and *Sheep May Safely Graze* are just two of the masterpieces found on this exceptional recording. By the way, tea came to

Germany in 1640 so it is possible that Bach may have had the opportunity to taste the hot beverage which would soon sweep Europe. If so, why didn't he write a "Tea Cantata" rather than his "Coffee Cantata"?

Recommended Recording: Parkening Plays Bach
Christopher Parkening, solo guitar, Angel CDC-7 471912

Blueberry Bars

These summer pastries are guaranteed to turn your fingers blue. Serve them slightly chilled and, if using your fingers, with a large napkin.

Crust ingredients
1 cup flour
1/2 cup butter, softened
1/2 cup confectioners' sugar

Preheat oven to 350 degrees F. Blend all ingredients and press into an 8 or 9-inch square pan. Bake for 15 minutes or until edges are just beginning to turn golden.

Filling ingredients
1 cup sour cream
1 egg, beaten
1 cup sugar
1 teaspoon vanilla
1/2 teaspoon almond extract
1/4 teaspoon salt
2 tablespoons flour
2 cups fresh blueberries

Combine sour cream, egg, sugar, vanilla, almond extract, flour and salt. Beat until smooth. Fold in blueberries. Pour over crust and bake at 400 degrees F. for 25 minutes.

Topping ingredients
3 tablespoons butter, softened
3 tablespoons flour
3 tablespoons sugar
1/4 cup sliced almonds

Combine all ingredients. Sprinkle over pie and bake 10 additional minutes. Chill before serving.

Onion Tart

Vidalia onions are the best choice for this savory tart. Many southern recipes simply refer to this dish as onion pie.

Crust ingredients
2/3 cup vegetable shortening
2 cups flour
1/2 teaspoon salt
3 tablespoons apple cider vinegar
5 tablespoons cream

Cut shortening into flour and salt until mixture resembles course meal. Add vinegar and cream until it just sticks together. Chill until ready to use.

Filling ingredients
5-6 medium sweet onions
2 tablespoons bacon drippings
2 eggs
1/2 teaspoon salt
1/8 teaspoon white pepper
1/4 teaspoon dry mustard
1 1/4 cup milk

Slice the onions into thick slices. Saute in bacon drippings until just tender. Try to keep the onions from separating as much as possible.

Preheat oven to 425 degrees F. Combine eggs, salt, pepper, and mustard in a sauce pan . Gradually add milk and cook over low heat until thickened. Arrange onions on the tart shell and cover with sauce. Sprinkle with parmesan cheese. Bake for 15 minutes, then reduce heat to 375 degrees F. and bake an additional 35-40 minutes or until set. Serves 6 for lunch or 8 for tea.

"Sunflowers" by
Holly VanMeter

Goldenrod Tea Sandwiches

We love the taste of apricots - both fresh and dried. Consequently, we use this versatile fruit in many recipes. The sweet flavor of apricots mixes well with cheese. This colorful recipe combines two of our favorite spreads to make a beautiful tea sandwich named after the Kentucky state flower.

Pimento cheese ingredients
1/2 pound very sharp cheddar cheese, grated
1/2 pound processed American cheese
1/4 cup mayonnaise
5 tablespoons sweet pickle juice
2 dashes cayenne pepper

Mix all ingredients in a food processor until blended. Mixture should be slightly lumpy. Refrigerate.

Apricot filling ingredients
1 cup dried apricots
2 cups water
1/2 cup sugar
8 ounces cream cheese
dash of salt

Add water to apricots and cook over medium heat until softened. Add sugar and continue to cook until some of the apricots begin to dissolve. Cool.

In a food processor, mix cream cheese, apricots, and a dash of salt. Refrigerate.

To assemble sandwiches, take 2 pieces of white bread and spread one with apricot filling. Spread pimento cheese on the other. Place a slice of whole wheat bread between the two fillings. Trim the crust and slice into 3 rectangle sandwiches.

Peach Preserves

Summer would be incomplete without the sweet taste of juicy summer peaches. Peach preserves are wonderful on scones, biscuits, toast, pancakes, or homemade ice cream.

4 cups fresh peaches, sliced and peeled
3 cups sugar
juice of 1 lemon

Put peaches in a large kettle. Add sugar and lemon juice. Simmer slowly until syrup becomes thick and peaches are slightly transparent. Skim off top when foam appears. Stir occasionally. Pour into sterilized jars and let cool for 24 hours. Seal with paraffin. Makes 2 pints.

Summer Cake

This warm weather cake is incredibly moist, and is always a favorite dessert.

3 sticks butter
3 cups sugar
5 eggs
3/4 cup milk
3 cups flour, sifted
1 cup coconut
1 teaspoon vanilla
1 teaspoon almond flavoring

Preheat oven to 325 degrees F. Cream butter with sugar. Add the eggs, one at a time, and beat well after each addition. Alternate adding the flour and milk. Fold in the salt and then the coconut. Add the vanilla and almond flavorings. Pour into a greased tube pan and bake for 1 1/2 hours. Cool 10 minutes and remove from pan. Cool on a rack. Split into two layers when completely cooled.

<u>Pineapple Curd Filling</u>
3 eggs
1/4 cup fresh lemon juice
1/2 cup unsalted butter, melted
1 cup sugar
1/2 cup crushed pineapple

In the top of a double boiler, beat eggs and sugar over boiling water. Stir in lemon juice and melted butter. Stir constantly until slightly thickened. Pour into a glass bowl to cool to room temperature. Fold in crushed pineapple. Chill. Spread a thin coating over the bottom layer of cake without letting it run down the sides. Replace top cake layer.

<u>Frosting</u>
8 ounces cream cheese, softened
16 ounces confectioners sugar
1/2 cup softened butter
dash of salt
1/4 cup Amaretto liqueur

Whip together first 3 ingredients until fluffy. Add salt and Amaretto and mix well. Spread completely over assembled cake. Refrigerate cake until ready to serve.

Sunflower Whole Wheat Scones

We make two versions of these scones, one with sunflower seeds and a sweeter one with cinnamon sugar sprinkled on top. Using whole wheat pastry flour instead of regular whole wheat flour makes for a lighter scone. Both are wonderful with homemade peach preserves.

1 3/4 cup whole wheat pastry flour
2 tablespoons sugar
1 teaspoon cream of tartar
1/2 teaspoon baking soda
1/4 teaspoon salt
6 tablespoons unsalted butter
1/2 cup plus 1 tablespoon sunflower seeds, roasted
1/2 cup buttermilk
1 egg
1 egg white, beaten

Preheat oven to 400 degrees F. Lightly grease a circle in the middle of a baking sheet.

In a large bowl, stir together the flour, sugar, cream of tartar, baking soda, and salt. Cut in the butter and mix until batter resembles coarse crumbs. Add the 1/2 cup sunflower seeds and stir. In a small bowl, mix together the buttermilk and egg. Add this mixture to the flour mix, combining just enough to moisten the flour. Pour the dough out onto a floured surface and shape into a round loaf. Score with a knife, making 8 triangles. Brush the top area with egg white and sprinkle with remaining sunflower seeds.

Place the loaf on a prepared baking sheet and bake for 15 minutes or until top is browned and a toothpick inserted in the center comes out clean. Options: To make a sweeter scone, top the loaf with cinnamon sugar. Individual round scones may also be made from this recipe by rolling out and cutting circles from the dough.

Nectarine Sorbet

The refreshing taste of frozen nectarines on a hot August day will have all your guests asking for the recipe to this simple dessert.

3-4 ripe nectarines
1 1/2 cups simple syrup

Use the simple syrup recipe found in the Basics section of this book. Chop the nectarines and remove the seeds. Process the ingredients in a blender and process at high speed. Pour the mixture into a bowl and place in a freezer. Stir twice at 30 minute intervals. Freeze completely. Scoop out into glass serving dishes.

Fall, by Irina Ilina

FALL

September - Tea at the Ballet

October - Kentucky Harvest Tea

November - Tea with Monet

Tea at the Ballet

Featured tea: Harney & Sons Russian Caravan
Whole Wheat Blini with Sour Cream and Caviar
New Potatoes stuffed with Ham
Cream Puff Swans
Pavlova
Fresh Berries and Honey

Ballet had its beginning in Italy 500 years ago. Taken from the Italian word ballare - to dance - our modern day ballroom has its roots in that tradition. It was Catherine de Medici who brought her love for dancing to the French court when she became Queen of France. The new artform flourished under her patronage and ballet positions to this day have French names.

Some of the world's best known ballets are from the Russian repertoire. Greatest of all Russian ballet composers was Piotr Ilyich Tchaikovsky, whose Swan Lake, Sleeping Beauty and The Nutcracker dominated the world stage in the second half of the 19th century.

The Russian thirst for tea goes back to 1638 when a gift of 140 pounds of tea was delivered to the court of Czar Mikhail Fedorovich. It took two centuries for the new beverage to find its way into the average Russian's home. But by the mid 1900's, Russian tea was all the rage in Paris.

The spread of tea throughout Russia was accompanied by the production of the samovar. Made of either bronze or copper, this tall common utensil keeps water hot all day long with its charcoal hot air system. A small teapot filled with concentrated tea sits on top and hot water is drawn from a spigot to dilute the tea as it is poured into a glass with a metal handle. Russians drink either black or green tea, often sweetened by a lump of sugar which is placed between the teeth and the gums. "Ecstasy," wrote Pushkin, " is a glass of tea and a piece of sugar in the mouth..."

Our Tea at the Ballet has a strong Russian influence. Russian artist, Irina Ilina, has painted a flowing portrait of a Russian ballerina to accompany our setting. A quartet of cream puff swans eyes the caviar-laden blinis nearby as our samovar delivers steaming hot tea for our guests. This tea with a Russian flair is the perfect prelude to an evening at the ballet or, better yet, a sweet distraction during one of the long intermissions.

Recommended recording: Tchaikovsky at Tea Time
An outstanding compilation of best-known selections from Piotr Ilyich Tchaikovsky ballets: Swan Lake, Sleeping Beauty, and The Nutcracker Suite. Orchestras include St. Martins in Fields and The Boston Symphony. Phillips 454 498-2

New Potatoes Stuffed with Ham

These tiny potatoes are filled with chopped ham and topped with Gruyere cheese. They can be made well ahead of your event.

15-20 small new potatoes, similar in size
1 cup finely chopped ham
1 tablespoon Dijon mustard
1 cup grated Gruyere cheese
green onion tops

Wash the potatoes. Place them in a large kettle with enough water to cover. Add 1 tablespoon salt. Bring to a boil and cook until just done, 20-30 minutes. Drain and cool. Cut 1/3 of the top of each potato. With a melon scoop or tomato shark, scoop out each piece leaving enough potato to allow each section to stand on its own. In a food processor, mix ham and mustard. Spread the mixture in the bottom of each potato boat and top with cheese and a few julienne green onion strips.

Pavlova

This spectacular dessert was named for the most famous Russian ballerina of the twentieth century. Anna Pavlova mesmerized audiences worldwide with her trademark "The Dying Swan" danced to the music of Camille Saint-Saens. Tradition has it that a recipe similar to this one was created in her honor by a New York restaurant.

8 egg whites, room temperature
1 3/4 cups granulated sugar
1/2 teaspoon cream of tartar
8 teaspoons cornstarch
3 teaspoons vinegar
2 teaspoons vanilla
1 pint heavy cream, whipped
fresh sliced strawberries, raspberries, or peaches

Preheat oven to 250 degrees F. Beat egg whites and cream of tartar until stiff. Gradually add sugar while beating, a little at a time, until mixture is glossy. Beat in cornstarch, vinegar, and vanilla. Lightly grease a baking pan or cookie sheet and cover with parchment paper. Pour the stiff egg whites out onto the paper, forming a mound. Shape this into a large circle and make a depression in the middle of the mound. The surrounding edges should be higher than the middle. Bake for 1 1/2 hours or until the meringue is firm and slightly brown. Turn off the heat and allow the Pavlova to remain in the oven for an additional hour. Remove from the oven and peel the paper off the bottom. Place the cooled Pavlova on a beautiful flat serving plate. When ready to serve, mound the whipped cream into the middle and decorate the top with fresh fruit. The center of the Pavlova will remain moist inside which makes it different from a meringue. Serves 8-10.

Whole Wheat Blini with Sour Cream and Caviar

Blinis are the Russian equivalent of Mexican tortillas. Larger ones are used to hold a variety of fillings while our smaller version is topped with sour cream and caviar.

1 cup milk
1/2 teaspoon yeast
1/2 teaspoon sugar
4 eggs, separated
1/2 teaspoon salt
3 tablespoons melted butter
1 cup whole wheat flour
1/2 cup all-purpose flour

Scald the milk, then cool to lukewarm. Add yeast, sugar, and salt to the milk. Beat the egg yolks and butter; add to yeast mixture. Now add flour. Cover and let rise in a warm place for 90 minutes.

Beat the egg whites until stiff. Fold them into the flour/yeast mixture. Mix thoroughly. Heat a lightly greased griddle until it is hot. Drop tablespoons of batter onto the griddle and cook until golden, turn and cook until the other side is brown. Keep warm until all are cooked. Blinis may be wrapped in foil and stored in the refrigerator for later use. Reheat at 300 degrees F. for 10 minutes. Top warm blinis with a dollop of sour cream, topped with a small amount of caviar and a sprig of dill. Makes 25-30.

Cream Puff Swans

Swans are a common theme in ballet story lines. Maybe it is because their graceful movements are so imitable. These easy-to-make swan-like cream puffs will certainly impress your tea time guests.

1 cup water
4 tablespoons unsalted butter
dash of salt
1 cup flour
4 eggs

Bring water, butter, and salt to a boil in a saucepan. After the butter has melted, add the flour. Mix quickly with a wooden spoon until batter is smooth. Continue to stir for a few minutes over low heat in order to dry the dough. The dough should not stick to your fingers when touched. Transfer the dough to a clean bowl and let it cool. Add eggs, one at a time, until mixture is smooth. Grease and flour a cookie sheet. Using about 3/4 of the dough, drop large tablespoons of dough (2" diameter) onto the prepared sheet.

Place the remaining batter into a pastry tube fitted with a large round tip. Pipe the batter onto a prepared baking sheet in the shape of an "S". Brush all the dough shapes with beaten egg and let dry for 25 minutes.

Preheat oven to 370 degrees F. Bake for 30-35 minutes or until light brown. Turn off heat, open the oven door slightly, and let the puffs cool in the oven for 20 minutes. Cool completely before use.

Filling
2 cups heavy cream
1/2 cups sugar
1 tablespoon cognac vanilla

Whip the heavy cream until slightly thickened. Add sugar and continue whipping until the cream is thick. Fold in the vanilla.

To assemble: Split the puffs in half horizontally. Then split the top in half in order to make wings. Fill the bottom half with cream. Place an "S" into the cream for a neck and head. Add the wings. Refrigerate until ready to serve. Makes 8-12 swans.

Cream Puff Swans

Fresh Berries and Honey

This simple combination of fresh fruits and golden honey makes a light finale for our Russian ballet tea.

fresh blackberries
fresh strawberries
fresh blueberries
honey

Wash and drain the fresh berries. Mix together and place in a glass bowl or compote. Drizzle honey over the top. Allow your guests to serve themselves. Place a glass bowl of honey next to the fruit in case someone would like extra sweetness.

Kentucky Harvest Tea

Tea Selection: Elmwood Inn Orange and Spice
Bourbon Balls
Miniature Transparent Pies
Shaker Lemon Tarts
Country Ham Pate with Corn Muffins
Cherry Tomatoes Stuffed with Minted Peas
Hot Brown Tarts
Elmwood Inn Woodford Pudding with Blackberry Brandy Sauce

Kentucky is a state of definite seasons, each with its particular palette of colors, aromas, sights, and sounds. Fall in Kentucky is one of our most spectacular seasons with brilliant forests of bright orange and red maples, fields of drying corn, pumpkins ripening on the vine, and countless festivals taking place in almost every county and country crossroad.

The ancient trees in the Elmwood Inn lawn are ablaze with color. The setting afternoon sun shimmers off the yellow leaves of our Ginkgo tree standing near the river. It will quickly shed its coat one morning in a continuous shower of cascading leaves which almost covers up the squirrels scurrying about, hiding their winter store of acorns.

A chill in the air as the sun begins to wane prompts you to fill the kettle and have a cup of hot tea in the late afternoon. Our fall tea table is spread with traditional foods common to Kentucky kitchens. Country ham, the last cherry tomatoes from the withering vines, tiny tarts, warm puddings, and chocolate balls laced with a splash of Bourbon make a savory and sweet combination which entices our visitors to return year after year.

Accompanying this autumn celebration is our featured tea, Orange and Spice. This is a favorite fall tea of our regular guests at the inn. We blend a black China tea with bits of dried orange peel and spices. The gentle citrus aroma meets your nose long before the delicious liquid touches your lips.

The relaxing strains of the dulcimer are often heard at Kentucky fall festivals. This celtic-based instrument has long been a standard instrument of the Kentucky mountain region and now dulcimer clubs have sprung up all over the state as more and more folk music enthusiasts are drawn to its magical sound. We have a beautiful Kentucky-made hammer-dulcimer here at the inn. We hope to someday learn how to play it. In the meantime, we like to listen to Maggie Sansone's recordings of the best Celtic/ Appalachian folk tunes. You will hear her recordings being played in many of the shops in nearby Berea, folk craft capitol of Kentucky.

Recommended recording: Mist and Stone. A collection of traditional hammer-dulcimer music performed by Maggie Sansone and friends. Maggie's Music MM 106

Bourbon Balls

No festive gathering in the Bluegrass region of Central Kentucky is complete without traditional Bourbon balls. These delicious confections should be made the day before your event. We prefer a mellow premium Bourbon.

1 stick of softened sweet butter
2 pounds confectioners' sugar
1/2 cup premium Bourbon
8 ounces semi-sweet chocolate
3 ounces unsweetened chocolate
1/2 rectangle paraffin

Mix the butter, sugar, and bourbon. Chill well. When cold, hand roll the candy into 1-inch balls. Place balls on cookie sheet and chill again. Melt the chocolate and paraffin in a double boiler. When smooth, dip the chilled balls into chocolate. Place a pecan half on top before the chocolate hardens. Store in an air-tight container in the refrigerator. Makes 24-30.

Transparent Pies

Transparent pies are found in almost every cookbook written about authentic Kentucky cuisine. They are sometimes called transparent puddings. Ours are bitesize tarts which gives you the added flexibility of serving them at parties. This recipe was brought to our attention by Margaret Thompson, a retired home economist from Georgetown, Kentucky.

3-4 ounces tart raspberry jelly
1/2 cup butter, softened
2 eggs, well beaten
1/4 cup sugar
1/4 cup brown sugar

Preheat oven to 400 degrees F. Line 4 mini-muffin tins with a small amount of pastry dough. Refer to the pastry recipe found in the Basics section of this book. Bake for 5 minutes or just until the crust is done, not browned. Remove from the oven. Place a small amount of jelly in the bottom of each shell.

Cream the butter with the sugars, then lightly beat in the eggs. Spread a spoonful of this mixture over the jelly in each shell. Reduce the oven to 350 degrees F. and bake for 5-7 minutes or until the top is set. Do not overcook. Remove from oven and cool completely in tins. Makes 4 dozen.

Shaker Lemon Tarts

The beautiful restored Shaker village of Pleasant Hill is just a few minutes away from Elmwood Inn. We have spent many peaceful hours walking its rolling fields and enjoying their bountiful Shaker meals. One of the traditional Shaker desserts is the terrifically tart Shaker pie. We have adapted the recipe to make miniature tarts, suitable for afternoon tea or receptions.

1 large lemon
2 eggs, well beaten
1 cup sugar

Slice the lemon, paper thin, into a bowl. Add the sugar, mix well and let stand for 2 hours at room temperature.

Preheat oven to 400 degrees F. Line 4 mini-muffin tins with a small amount of pastry dough. You will find a pastry recipe in the Basics section of this book. Bake for 5 minutes or just until the crust is done, not browned. Remove from the oven.

Add the beaten eggs to the lemon mixture and stir well. Pour the mixture into a blender and pulse a few times to chop the lemons. Pour the mixture back into a bowl. Spoon a small amount of the filling into each crust and bake for 5-7 minutes at 350 degrees F. Remove the tins from the oven and cool completely before removing the tarts from the pans. Makes about 4 dozen.

Country Ham Pate

This satisfying spread will delight your hungry guests who love savory finger food. You may spread it liberally on biscuits or, our preference, corn muffins.

5 dill pickle spears
2 green onions, chopped
1/4 cup chopped parsley
1 1/2 teaspoons fresh or dried tarragon
1/2 teaspoon marjoram
2 tablespoons coarse country Dijon mustard
1 pound cooked country ham, sliced thin
Tabasco or hot pepper sauce, to taste

In a food processor, combine pickles, onions, herbs, and mustard on high setting. Using a knife, chop the ham and add it to the processor. Add a few drops of hot sauce and process until the mixture holds together and is spreadable.

Place the mixture into a mold and refrigerate until ready to serve. Turn the molded pate out onto a serving stand and garnish with fresh parsley. Serve with corn muffins.

Corn Muffins

The historic Weisenberger Mills in Midway has been in operation for over a century amid the immaculate thoroughbred horse farms of Woodford County. They produce our scone mix and shortbread mix, but are best known for their wonderful yellow corn meal and baking flours.

3/4 cup flour
3/4 cup yellow corn meal
2 teaspoons baking powder
1/2 teaspoon salt
2 tablespoons sugar
2 tablespoons melted butter
3/4 cup whole milk
1 egg dash of cayenne pepper

Preheat oven to 450 degrees F. Mix dry ingredients in a large bowl. In a separate bowl, mix the melted butter, milk, and egg. Add the egg mixture to the dry ingredients and stir until just mixed. Pour the batter into a greased muffin tin until each cup is 2/3 full. Bake for 8-12 minutes for small muffins or 10-15 minutes for large muffins. Makes 36 small or 18 regular size muffins.

Cherry Tomatoes Stuffed with Minted Peas

Our late summer cherry tomato vines often are bearing their last fruits as the month of October comes in. It is always a challenge to find a good use for all those tiny sweet tomatoes. Here is a recipe which makes good use of them while providing a natural cup for our minted peas.

2 cups fresh or frozen peas
1/4 cup fresh mint, chopped
1/2 teaspoon salt
1 teaspoon sugar
1 teaspoon butter
15-20 cherry tomatoes

Cook the peas with 1/2 cup water, salt, sugar, and butter. Bring to a boil and add the mint leaves. Cook the peas until they are just becoming soft, but not split. Drain and allow to cool. Cut the top 1/4 off of each tomato and scoop out the inside to make a cup. Turn over on a paper to towel and drain. Spoon the cooled peas into each tomato and top with fresh chopped mint leaves. Serve at room temperature or chill for later use.

Hot Brown Tart

The Hot Brown was originally introduced at the Brown Hotel in Louisville. Every Kentucky hostess knows how to make this traditional dish. Our adaptation of the recipe allows you to make small individual tarts which are the perfect size for an afternoon tea.

4 eggs
2 cups half and half
1/2 teaspoon salt
1/4 teaspoon pepper
1 cup chopped turkey breast, cooked
1/2 cup grated cheddar cheese
1/4 cup grated fresh Parmesan cheese
2 small tomatoes, sliced thin
4 slices crisp cooked bacon, crumbled

Preheat oven to 400 degrees F. Line a 9-inch tart pan with pastry dough. You will find a pastry recipe in the Basics section of this book. Bake for 5-10 minutes or until crust is done, but not brown.

Beat the eggs and mix with half and half, salt, and pepper. Set aside. Place the chopped turkey breast on the tart crust and top with cheddar cheese. Pour the egg mixture over the cheese and then add tomatoes. Top with bacon and Parmesan cheese. Bake for 10 minutes at 400 degrees F., then reduce the temperature to 350 degrees F. and bake an additional 30 minutes or until a knife inserted in the middle comes out clean. The top should be brown and crusty. Remove the tart from the oven and cool before serving.

Elmwood Inn Woodford Pudding

This old Kentucky recipe is similar to an English jam pudding. It may have gotten its name from Woodford County where the countryside and rock fences resemble the Cotswalds of England. Woodford County is special to us because it was the site of our first home when we were married.

1/2 cup softened butter
3/4 cup sugar
3 eggs, separated
1 cup blackberry preserves
3/4 cup whole milk
1/2 cup flour
1/2 cup whole wheat flour
2 teaspoons baking powder
dash of salt
1 teaspoon vanilla
1 teaspoon cinnamon
1/2 teaspoon freshly grated nutmeg
1/4 teaspoon ground cloves

Preheat oven to 350 degrees F. Cream butter and sugar. Add egg yolks, vanilla, and preserves. Combine flour, baking powder, salt, and spices. Add flour mixture, alternating with milk. Begin and end this step with flour. Beat the egg whites until stiff. Gently fold the whites into the flour mixture. Pour into a greased mold or Pyrex dish. Bake for 30-35 minutes. Serve warm with Blackberry Brandy Sauce.

Blackberry Brandy Sauce

Pour this delicious sauce liberally over Woodford pudding, bread pudding, or fresh homemade vanilla ice cream.

1/4 cup softened butter
1/4 cup sugar
1 egg
2 tablespoons blackberry brandy
1/4 cup fresh or frozen blackberries

Cream the butter and sugar. Add egg and beat hard. Cook over medium heat, stirring constantly until mixture thickens. Do not boil. Remove from heat and add brandy and blackberries. Serve warm over Woodford Pudding.

Afternoon Tea with Claude Monet

Featured Tea: Harney & Sons Verveine Odorante

Petite boules de fromage

(Little mixed cheese balls)

Poulet et vinaigrette d'asperges

(Chicken and asparagus in vinaigrette)

Quiche aux courgettes

(Zucchini quiche)

Scones avec

Conserves de cerises

(Scones with cherry preserves)

Tartelette aux fraises du bois

(Wild strawberry tartlet)

Tartes aux poires

(Pear tart)

Pain de Genes

(Genoa Cake)

Sorbet a citron

(Lemon sorbet)

Truffles

One of the most influential painters of modern times, Claude Monet lived for half his life at his famous house and gardens at Giverny, France. It was after moving there in 1883 with his second wife, Alice, and their eight children that Monet's work finally achieved recognition. Fellow impressionists - Renoir, Pissarro, Sisley, Degas - often came to dine with the family in almost ritual form. They began with a stroll through Monet's spectacular gardens, had lunch at 11:30, visited the artist in his studio, and then enjoyed afternoon tea by the lily pond.

Our interest in Monet's art peaked while visiting the 1995 Monet Exhibition at the Art Institute of Chicago. This showing was the largest exhibit of Monet's works ever put together under one roof. *Monet Mania* swept through the Midwest as art lovers gathered in the Windy City for this impressionistic feast. After discovering the artist's cooking journals (*Monet's Table* by Claire Joyes), we knew we had to bring back some of this colorful excitement to Kentucky. Local artist, Rudy Ayoroa, painted a copy of Monet's *The Promenade* to hang prominently over our tea room mantle. Through the assistance of Lexington's Julia's Gallery, we were able to bring in scenes from Giverny by California artist and Giverny gardens expert, Elizabeth Murray. It was a wonderful blending of French cuisine, tea, and art.

Our featured tea is actually a herbal tisane because it contains no tea leaf. Imported from France, this mellow herb is similar to lemon verbena. The big green leaves, now dried, produce an unusually full-bodied yellow brew with a wonderful aroma. This is a great substitute for after-dinner coffee, and it won't keep your guests awake all night.

Our recommended recording is by French composer and Monet contemporary, Claude Debussy. Both artists shared a great love for the sea. It was often the inspiration for their best work. Debussy had the ability to see images with an impressionist's eye, and to work with the color and mass of instrumental combinations much as a painter works with pigments. For Debussy, his palette was the orchestra.

Recommended recording: *Prelude to the Afternoon of a Faun; The Sea/Claude Debussy*; **Montreal Symphony Orchestra/Charles Dutoit, London 425 502-2**

Wild Strawberry Tart

The European strawberry Charles V is the preferred berry for this classic pastry; however, any fresh strawberry may be used. Try to hand select firm berries of uniform size.

Pastry ingredients
1 cup flour
1/4 pound butter, softened
2 tablespoons confectioners sugar
3 tablespoons finely chopped pecans or almonds

Preheat oven to 375 degrees F. Cut flour, sugar, and butter together. Add nuts and press into a 9-inch tart pan. Bake for 12 minutes or until just golden.

Filling ingredients
8 ounces cream cheese
1/2 cup sugar
2 tablespoons cream
2 tablespoons Grand Marnier
zest of 1 orange

Cream all ingredients together. Spoon into cooled crust and chill.

Topping ingredients
1 pint fresh strawberries (uniform in size)
1 cup red currant jelly

Slice strawberries in half and place on top the cream filling around the edge of the tart shell. Melt jelly in a saucepan and allow to cool. Glaze berries and cream cheese mixture. Chill.

Chicken and Asparagus Tea Sandwich

This unusual tea sandwich also works well as an appetizer before a dinner party.

2 tablespoons lemon juice
1/4 cup olive oil
1/4 cup safflower oil
2 tablespoons sherry vinegar
1/2 teaspoon salt
1/4 teaspoon pepper
2-4 teaspoons red wine vinegar
1 box frozen chopped asparagus
3-4 cooked chicken breasts, diced
3 tablespoons melted butter
white bread

Whisk together vinegars, oil, and lemon juice. Add salt and pepper. Set aside.

Cook asparagus according to package directions. Cool and drain. Place chicken, asparagus, and vinaigrette in food processor. Process until just blended. Refrigerate.

Make toast triangles by removing crust from a good white bread. Dredge in melted butter or margarine and bake on a cookie sheet in a 250 degree oven until gold brown. Cool. Place asparagus mixture on toast and serve.

Zucchini Quiche

Afternoon tea at Elmwood Inn almost always includes a quiche. The savory flavor of these individual baked tarts gives balance to the sweetness of the courses yet to come.

Pastry ingredients
1 1/2 cups all-purpose flour
1/4 teaspoon salt
1 stick cold butter
5 tablespoons cold water

Combine flour and salt. Cut in butter and blend with a pastry blender until mixture resembles coarse crumbs. Add enough water to form the mixture into a ball. Wrap in plastic wrap and chill for 30 minutes.

Preheat oven to 425 degrees F. Roll out dough on a floured board and fit into a 9-inch tart pan. Line pastry shell with wax paper and fill with one layer of dried beans to keep the crust flat while baking. Bake for 10 minutes. Remove beans and paper. Reduce temperature to 375 and continue to bake for 5-7 minutes. Remove from oven and cool.

Filling ingredients
3 small tender zucchini
2 tablespoons unsalted butter
1 clove garlic, minced
1 cup half and half
3 large eggs
1 tablespoon chopped fresh oregano
1 tablespoon chopped fresh basil
1 tablespoon chopped fresh chervil
freshly grated nutmeg (to taste)
salt (to taste)
pepper (to taste)

Trim and cut zucchini into 1/2-inch thick slices. Blanch in a large saucepan of boiling salted water for 1 minute. Drain and plunge into cold water. Drain once again and pat dry. Preheat oven to 350 degrees F.

Melt butter in skillet. Add garlic and cook over medium heat for one minute. Add zucchini. Stir and cook for 5 minutes. Arrange mixture in pastry shell.

Combine half and half, eggs, herbs, nutmeg, salt, and pepper. Whisk together and pour mixture over zucchini. Bake for 45-50 minutes. Serves 4 to 6.

Giverny Scones

Tea and scones are the perfect combination for a light afternoon tea — a British tradition enjoyed regularly in the gardens of Giverny.

2 cups flour
1 teaspoon baking powder
1/4 teaspoon salt
6 ounces buttermilk
4 tablespoons butter
1 egg white for glaze

Preheat oven to 400 degrees F. Sift together flour, baking powder, and salt. Cut in butter with a pastry blender until mixture resembles coarse crumbs. Add buttermilk to make a soft dough. Roll dough out on a floured board to a 1/2-inch thickness. Cut out circles with a round fluted biscuit cutter. Brush tops of scones with egg white. Bake for 15 minutes or until lightly browned. Serve hot, slicing and spreading with cherry preserves. Makes 15-20 small scones.

"Wisteria Covered Footbridge" by Elizabeth Murray

Cherry Preserves

Cherries, plums, and red currants were all popular fruits which found their way to the Monet table by way of his blue-tiled kitchen. You can still visit the famous house and gardens just west of Paris. Don't miss the water lilies!

4 cups chopped sour cherries (pitted)
4 3/4 cups sugar
1 box sure gel

Combine cherries and gel in a large pot. Bring to a full, rolling boil. Stir constantly. Add sugar and return to boil for one minute. Continue to stir. Remove from heat and pour into prepared canning jars. Seal lids as described in the lid maker's instructions.

Pear Tart

French pastry chefs are known for their creative use of fruit to decorate fine pastries and tarts. This traditional dessert will please the eye - as well as the palate - of your guests.

4-5 peeled pears
2 1/2 quarts water
5 cups sugar
1 orange or lemon
1 cinnamon stick

Bring water and sugar to a rolling boil. Add rind of 1 orange or lemon which has been removed in 1 or 2 large pieces. Add 1 stick cinnamon. Continue to boil. Place peeled pears, cored and halved, into the water. Cook over medium heat until slightly transparent. Carefully remove from poaching liquid with a slotted spoon. Drain and cool. Reserve liquid.

2 cups flour
2/3 cup shortening
3 tablespoons apple cider vinegar
3 tablespoons heavy cream
dash of salt

Cut shortening into flour and salt until the mixture resembles coarse meal. Add vinegar and cream to make the dough stick together. Refrigerate. Makes 2 crusts. When ready to use, roll out on a lightly floured board until about 1/8 inch thick. Carefully fit into a 9-inch tart pan. Chill until ready to fill.

1 stick unsalted butter
1/2 cup sugar
1 egg
1 cup finely ground almonds
3 tablespoons dark rum
1 teaspoon almond extract
1 tablespoon all-purpose flour

Cream together butter and sugar until light and fluffy. Add egg, almonds, rum, almond extract, and flour. Mix well. Spread on chilled tart crust. Preheat oven to 425 degrees F. Place cooled pears on a board. With the bottom of the pear facing you, make cuts from bottom to top, slicing all the way through on the right side only. Leave the left side hinged. This allows you to fan the pears out on top of the tart filling. Place the small end of the pear toward the middle of the tart so that the overall design resembles a blooming flower. Bake for 40-50 minutes or until golden brown.

While tart is baking, reduce 1 cup of poaching liquid by one-half. Add rum. When tart is pulled from the oven, brush pears with glaze. Serve barely warm or at room temperature.

Pear Tart

Lemon Sorbet

This light refreshment is the perfect ending to a beautiful tea. Color and presentation are as important as taste in the enjoyment of a fine meal. Colorful depression glass goblets on lace doilies help make this a visual feast.

2 cups water
1 cup sugar
juice of 6 large lemons

Bring water and sugar to boil in saucepan until syrup is formed. Cool completely. Stir in lemon juice. Pour into a stainless steel bowl and place in freezer for one hour. Whisk and return to freezer. Continue to whisk at 30 minute intervals until firm (about 3 hours total). Cover and keep frozen until ready to serve.

Genoa Cake

This was one of Claude Monet's favorite cakes. Here is Elmwood's adaptation of this classic sweet tea cake.

1/2 cup unsalted butter, room temperature
1 1/2 cup confectioners sugar
5 eggs
2 1/4 cups ground almonds
3 tablespoons orange marmalade
2/3 cup flour
1/2 cup sifted confectioner's sugar
1/2 cup slivered almonds (toasted)

Preheat oven to 350 degrees F. Grease an 8-inch round cake pan. In a medium bowl, cream butter and sugar until fluffy. Mix in eggs, one at a time mixing well after each addition. Beat in ground almonds along with marmalade. Add flour and beat well.

Pour batter into prepared cake pan and bake for 40 minutes or until golden. Cool in pan for 15 minutes, then turn out on to rack. Cool completely. Place on a beautiful cake plate, top with almonds, then sprinkle with confectioner's sugar.

Truffles

These deep chocolate delights are eagerly anticipated by our guests. They are a chocoholic's dream.

1 cup cream
3 tablespoons Grand Marnier, Kahlua, or Amaretto
6 ounces semi-sweet chocolate
6 ounces sweet chocolate
8 tablespoons unsalted butter, softened
confectioners' sugar
unsweetened Dutch process powdered cocoa

Bring cream to a boil and reduce to 1/2 cup. Add liqueur and chocolate. Stir over low heat until chocolate melts. Whisk in soft butter and mix until smooth. Pour into a bowl and refrigerate until firm.

Use a small melon scoop to shape the chocolate mixture into balls. Roll half of each ball in confectioners' sugar and half in cocoa. Line a covered tin or plastic container with wax paper and store truffles in refrigerator. Makes 50.

Basics

Several basic recipes are used repeatedly this book. You'll find them listed below.

Pastry Crust

This dough is called for in tart shells and pie crusts. Keep it chilled in the refrigerator until ready to use.

1 1/2 cup flour
1/2 teaspoon salt
2 tablespoons butter
1/3 cup shortening
2-3 tablespoons ice-cold water

Mix together the flour and salt. Cut in the shortening and butter until coarse crumbs form. Sprinkle in water while mixing lightly. Form the dough into a ball. Chill before rolling out.

Rose Water

Always use organically-grown rose petals for this summertime staple.

1 quart water
2 cups fresh rose petals

Bring 1 quart of water to a full boil. Pour the heated water over 2 cups of fresh rose petals. Store in a glass jar with a lid. When cooled, strain out the petals. Refrigerate until ready to use.

Simple Syrup

This sweet syrup is called for in a number of recipes. You may keep it stored in the refrigerator for up two weeks.

1 cup sugar
2 cups water

Bring sugar and water to a boil. Pour into a container and refrigerate until ready to use.

INDEX OF RECIPES

Tea Suppliers

Elmwood Inn Fine Teas
205 East Fourth Street
Perryville, KY 40468
606-332-2400
www.elmwoodinn.com
Wholesale and retail teas, scone mix, shortbread
mix, lemon curd,cranberry curd, decorated sugars,
and tea books. Afternoon tea is served Thursday,
Friday, and Saturday with seatings at 1:00 and
3:00. Reservations are advised.

Harney & Sons Fine Teas
PO Box 638
Salisbury, CT 06068
800-TEATIME
Wholesale and retail teas, brewing equipment,
and tea gifts.

Donna & Ron Lasko
140 Main Street
Osterville, MA 02655
508-428-2128
Retail suppliers of Courtship Tea.

Featured Artists

Irina Ilina
c/o Elmwood Inn
205 E. Fourth Street
Perryville, Kentucky 4068
Specializing in watercolors, porcelains, and fine
jewelry.

Holly VanMeter
339 Burns
Winchester, Kentucky 40391
Specializing in still-life watercolors.

Debbie Wheat
c/o Elmwood Inn
205 East Fourth Street
Perryville, Kentucky 40422
Specializing in period floorcloths.

Music

All of the compact discs recommended in this
book may be ordered by calling
1-800-75-MUSIC. A portion of each sale will go
toward the support of your local National Public
Radio station.

Music by Maggie Sansone may be ordered by
calling Maggie's Music at 410-268-3394.